DEEP SOUTH - DEEP NORTH
A FAMILY'S JOURNEY

by Lottie B. Scott

DORRANCE
PUBLISHING CO
EST. 1920
PITTSBURGH, PENNSYLVANIA 15238

Dorrance Publishing Co
585 Alpha Drive
Pittsburgh, PA 15238
Visit our website at *www.dorrancebookstore.com*

ISBN: 978-1-4809-6034-3
eISBN: 978-1-4809-6057-2

CONTENTS

Preface

A Mother's Love Inspired Generations

This book is dedicated to our mother, Estelle Stone Bell, who showed us the way through the storms of hardships. She taught us honesty. She taught us that hard work would not kill us but would make us strong. She told us to work for what we wanted and not depend upon others. She taught us compassion and how to love without saying the word.

During our beginnings, we were poor and humble, but we had and still possess a great spirit within us that has helped us make a way when none seemed possible. Our success must be measured not by our current material possessions, but by the odds we had to overcome to be where we are today.

What follows are struggles, accomplishments, and triumphs of eight children growing up with their parents on a farm in Longtown, South Carolina: four brothers and four sisters, a mother, and a father surrounded by poverty, prejudice, and racial segregation.

This book is a gift to the descendants of Joe Bell, Jr. and Estelle Stone Bell, their children, grandchildren, great-grandchildren, great-great-grandchildren, and future generations. A people should know their history. Our story serves as footprints of our past. May future generations find these footprints helpful as they chart their own course.

A great people is not ashamed of its past. The past becomes the building blocks for those who follow, and so it shall be with our family.

ACKNOWLEGEMENTS

I would like to express my great appreciation to my best friend, Clifford Carter, Jr., to my son, Clyburn Scott Jr., and grandson, Clyburn Scott III for their valuable support and encouragement during the writing of this book.

I would like to express a special thank you to Jeffrey Isben, Thomasina Clemons, Grace Sawyer Jones, Michael Bradford, Maura Casey and Shiela Hayes, who provided support, offered comments, and assisted in the editing, proofreading and design. A special thanks to Cora Hayward and Jeanne Zuzel for more than twenty-five years of sharing their gifts on natural healing.

I would also like to thank Geneva B. Bell, Joe Belton, Joe Benson, Tony Mae Bush Butler, Dianne Daniels, Henrietta Whitaker-Gibson, Derwin Jackson, Nancy Belton Ross Jackson, Thomas Jackson, Marilyn Jackson Jasmin, Lela B. Jones, Norvice B. Little, Gail McCool, Martha B. Marshall, George B. Murphy, Margaret K. Murphy, Luvenia Patterson, Josephine B. Patton, Lottie Mae Griffin Russell, Dinah Bell Stone, Luisa Stranges, Reecy Thompson, Alice White, and Alberta Williams. Also, I would like to thank family and friends of Longtown, South Carolina for their steadfast support over the years.

Finally, I would like to thank the many people who assisted and saw me through this book.

Chapter 1 — The Setting

Dating back to the 1800s, our paternal great-grandparents, Warren Bell and Nora Roach Bell, and George Belton and Alice Belton, and our maternal great-grandparents, William Stone and Janie Derry Stone, and George Goins and Charity Kirkland Goins, were raised in Kershaw and Fairfield Counties. Our paternal grandparents, Joe Bell Sr. and Dinah Belton Bell, and our maternal grandparents, Solomon Stone and Ella Goins Stone, were raised in Fairfield County. Our parents, Joe Bell Jr. and Estelle Stone Bell, were born and raised in rural Longtown, South Carolina. Kershaw and Fairfield Counties are adjacent to each other, and the Wateree River flows through both counties, allowing for easy social connection. The Wateree River served as a gateway to both counties dating back to the days of slavery. Ancestors told stories of leaving Liberty Hill, crossing the Wateree River to enter Kershaw County, and moving on to Fairfield County.

The Emancipation Proclamation was signed in 1863, and in 1866 four jubilant former slaves by the names of Lisbon White Sr., George Belton, Douglas Murphy, and Horace Lawhorne went from house to house to inform the community of their plans to build a church. In early 1867, according to local historian Alice White, a white man named John Robinson gave three acres of land upon which the church was erected. The church building was completed in April 1867, and it was named Rock Hill Baptist Church. While the men and women weren't of "letters," they could relate to rocks and hills from previous experiences. Services were held twice a month because of the long walking distance people had to travel to attend. Rock Hill Baptist Church, home church of George Goins and Charity Kirkland Goins, became the inspiration for the establishment of Mount Olive Baptist Church, Mount Pilgrim Baptist Church, and Antioch Baptist Church. Mount Olive Baptist Church was organized by Abram Brunson, George Butler, Julius Brevard, and Sony Brown Belton. They decided that five miles was too far for the children to walk to Sunday school, so between two sweet gum trees and two cedar posts, they erected a brush arbor, which became the church.

In 1884, another group of house workers led by Robert Murphy, including the Bells, Bensons, Burtons, Huckabees, Kiblers, Murphys, Nelsons, Peays, Portees, Roaches, Starks, and Williams, built First Methodist Church, which later was renamed Mount Joshua United Methodist Church, according to historian Alice White of Longtown, South Carolina. The church held its first service on May 3, 1884. It became the home church of our paternal great-grandparents, Warren and Nora Roach Bell, and their children, including Grandpa Joe Bell Sr., who married Dinah Belton, daughter of our great-grandparents George and Alice Belton.

In 1919, Daddy's mother, Grandma Dinah Belton, died following the birth of her youngest child, Della. She left behind six children: Daddy, Albert, Phillip, George, Mary Alice, and Della. Following their mother's death, Julia Briggs, who lived across the road from Grandpa Joe, assisted him with caring for the children. Some time later, Julia moved into Grandpa Joe's house and became his common-law wife. The children called her Julia, and their children called her Cuzin Julia.

Children calling adults by their first name was not the tradition in the South and why the children were allowed to call her Julia is a mystery to this day. Daddy was the sickly one because of a painful arm as a result of a fall when he was a very young child.

Mama's parents, Solomon Stone and Ella Goins Stone, had thirteen children, one stillborn named Eli. Mama was the seventh. The older daughters had married by the time Mama became old enough to work in the field. It was Mama, Scillar, and King Solomon who helped Grandpa Saul with the farming. Mama said the work was hard and Grandpa was a hard man to please. Mama learned a lot about farming from her brother King Solomon.

Our great-grandparents on both sides were landowners in Fairfield and Kershaw Counties. They planted vegetables, hunted, and fished as a way to provide for their families. While most of the farmland was owned by whites, some black families became owners of many acres of land as well. We were lucky in many ways as our parents controlled our going to school because our grandparents owned the land we worked. The children of sharecroppers had to receive permission from the white landowners as to when they could attend school. This was usually after all the cotton had been picked and harvest completed. We lived on Grandpa Joe's land, as did Uncle George and his family, who moved there after Grandpa Joe moved into a new house on the border of Fairfield and Kershaw Counties.

Our house was within walking distance to the Wateree River. We walked less than a mile through the woods to reach it. Mama sometimes would meet up with Daddy's Aunt Laura and together they would walk along the narrow unpaved red dirt road passing Antioch Baptist Church. The families were all farmers, but they would fish for hours whenever time permitted.

We lived in houses without electricity and within a stone's throw of our neighbors. When the sun went down, the lanterns came out.

There was a rush to get all work done by sundown. The chickens began their slow march to their coops to be placed out of harm's way. Stray dogs and foxes were always on the lookout for a meal. The farm animals were taken to the branch to get their last drink of water for the night. The hogs were fed. Children's playing ceased as parents stood outside yelling, "Come home now!" It was early to bed and early to rise. We would go to bed with the chickens and get up with the roosters. Once they began their cock-a-doodle-doing, there was no sleeping.

Sundays were church-going time. Parents walked miles to churches carrying children in their arms and around their shoulders, with little ones trotting to keep up. Walking or riding wagons were the only means of transportation at that time for our family.

As children, we enjoyed picking blackberries, yellow and red grapes, and black locust on our way to church. The sweet-tasting juice was a joy. We learned early to watch where to put our hands and feet, as the snakes loved the fruit as well. There also were plum trees along the road.

During the long walk along the red dusty roads, white fishermen terrorized us by driving within inches of our bodies, forcing us into the ditches and kicking up red dust. I recall the red dust sticking to my beautiful white starched dress, my black patent leather shoes, and my hair, which had been so carefully combed, lathered with pomade, and curled. Mama did her best to help me wipe the dust off my shoes, but there was no easy solution for removing it from my hair and dress, which were changed to shades of bright, glowing red. It was always a frightening experience while walking to church on a Sunday morning to serve a God of all the people. We prayed the men would miss us, but that rarely happened.

Chapter 2 — Mama Tells Me Stories

Mama began telling me stories at an early age about her life growing up in Longtown, South Carolina. She continued telling stories until about age eighty-five. When Mama began talking, you listened. She granted few interruptions. A few months after Mama and Daddy's marriage and before my birth, they moved into Uncle Chevis's little house, which was about a mile away from Grandpa Joe's place. Mama said it was frightening to be alone in the house after sundown and before sunrise.

As far back as I can remember, Mama said my nervousness and being sickly were the results of experiences she went through while she was pregnant with me. She told me that her nervousness was passed on to me while I was in her womb. Old wives' tales call this "marking" a child.

If I was late returning home from visiting with my friend Dot who lived within "hollering distance," Mama would remind me when I did not comply with her rule of returning home before sundown. She would begin telling me what would have happened to me in slavery time if I did not return home before sundown. Mama told how the slave masters would punish people if they did not return before sundown by beating them until blood ran down their backs. Then the master would hang them to the rafters all night and would not give them food. I asked Mama why people did not fight back. She replied, "Child, they would have beaten you more and half starved you to death. They had the power."

In an angry voice, I told Mama that I would have found a way to fight back: "I would have found a way to poison their food." Mama said, "No, no, child! Just because someone else is low-down, you don't have to be too." Then I told Mama how I would gather black people together and fight back. Mama shook her head and said, "Child, you would be killed. They got the power."

THE GROWING YEARS

CHAPTER 3 — THE BEGINNING

In the summer of 1936, Mama and Daddy were expecting their first child. They moved from the home of Grandpa Joe into a large, one-room wooden framed, dilapidated house once owned by Daddy's Uncle Chevis, brother of his deceased mother, Dinah. One section of the house was used for sleeping, the other part for daily living, cooking, and sitting. There also was a back porch and outside shed. The house was in very poor condition with boards off here and there. The little house was located within a stone's throw of the once large and stately home owned by Daddy's grandfather, George Belton, until his death in 1934. Both houses stood along the route to the Wateree River, commonly called "the Pond" by locals. Shortly after moving into the house, Mama found herself fighting chinch bugs daily and she heard loud banging noises against the house when she was alone. At times, the milk churn would be found on its side with milk spilling from it. She became frightened but said nothing to Daddy. Every day he would travel about a mile or so to his father's place where he would work from sunup until sundown. Mama was home alone. She was happy to see a few people going to and from the Pond. It was an opportunity to talk a little bit with them. Also, if the fishing was good, it was a chance someone would share a little of their catch. Fried fish or eel made a nice addition to their corn bread and milk dinner.

It was not long before Mama met Daddy's Aunt Laura while washing clothes at the spring, a gathering place where the women went weekly to wash clothes. Aunt Laura and Mama instantly became best friends, but there was only so much time the two could spend together, as Aunt Laura had a family to care for and work of her own to do.

One day while preparing dinner, Mama heard loud singing and laughing. She looked outside and saw a large crowd of people coming from the direction of the Pond heading up the road toward their house. Mama said it seemed to be taking them forever to get past the house, so she went inside to check again on the corn bread. When she returned within a few minutes, the people were nowhere in sight. Several days later, Mama again saw a large crowd of people singing and coming toward the house. She decided not to go inside but to wait. After two hours, the crowd of people continued to walk toward her, but never got any closer. She decided it was time to explore what was going on. She got up out of her chair, picked up her fishing pole, and started down the road in their direction to meet them and find out what was taking them so long.

As she approached Grandpa George Belton's house, Mama said, she began to hear organ music coming from inside. The music got louder and louder as she got closer. *No one is staying in that house!* she thought to herself. Missy, Grandpa George's wife, whom he married after Grandma Alice died, was the only one who could play the organ, and she was dead. Mama could still see a crowd of people coming toward her, but her attention was drawn to the music coming from inside Grandpa George's old house. She walked up to the window and peeked into the house, but she saw nothing. This did not surprise her because no one was living there. However, the organ music continued to play. She quietly opened the front door and tiptoed inside. She went from room to room looking for the music. Each room was empty except for spider webs and dust. Suddenly, the music stopped! Mama walked outside, expecting to see the crowd of people. There was no one. She looked up the road toward her house. There was no one in sight. The road was long and straight, and it was impossible for the crowd to disappear so quickly. She ran past her house and up the road, hoping to catch a glimpse of the people. She saw no one. Mama became frightened, and she remembered all the hant stories she had heard growing up. She did not believe the stories and attributed them to mere superstitions told to frighten children to keep them in line. She tried to reassure herself so that she would not be frightened, but deep down inside, she was shaking and afraid.

Mama did not tell Daddy of this incident. She waited until wash day and described the incidents to Aunt Laura, who was the youngest sister of Daddy's mother, Dinah. No sooner than the words left Mama's lips, Aunt Laura, in an angry voice, said, "There ain't nobody playing that organ but Old Missy. She used to play it when I lived there. When I got tired of her playing, I would tell her, 'I was not afraid of you when you were living, and I sure ain't afraid of you now.'" Aunt Laura told Mama that she would just go about her business, and Old Missy would eventually stop playing.

There seemed to have been no love between Old Missy and Grandpa George's children. It was rumored that Old Missy was one mean and hateful woman, as black and shiny as patent leather shoes, fat and ugly as homemade sin. Some said Missy promised to "piss and shit out" all of his money so there would be nothing left for his children. By the time Old Missy died, Grandpa George's fortune had greatly diminished. Some whisper that Missy kept her word. Others said that Grandpa George lost his wealth by his own doing: women and money.

Aunt Laura told Mama that the people she saw were hants who had been traveling that road since she was a child. She said, "She pays no attention to them," and that they never harmed her or anyone else. Aunt Laura continued, "Stell, when we were walking, did you ever feel a chill in spots of the road? Well, that is when we were meeting the hants. Did you ever notice that sometimes I would step aside? Well, we would be meeting a crowd of hants. Other times I would just walk right through them."

This revelation by Aunt Laura sent Mama into a panic. During the short time she had known Aunt Laura, Mama learned to trust her. However, she was not prepared to live with hants. She had to spend too much time alone. Mama was so frightened after that revelation, Aunt Laura had to turn around and walk her home. This process of turning around and walking another home was a ritual among girls and women that seemed to have been passed down from one generation to another. Each girl or woman would take turns walking the other one part of the way home. This going back and forth between them could go on for hours, if time permitted. Aunt Laura could not be with Mama all the time and Daddy had to travel to his father's place to work. So Mama began to take Dr. Miles' Nervine medicine daily to help calm her nerves.

Mama was looking forward to the birth of their first child. During the day, she spent her time making baby clothes from flour sacks and pieces of scrap cloth. As the sun journeyed westward, passing over the tall pine trees, and a golden horizon slowly peeked above the trees, Mama would sing. She was happy knowing Daddy would be home soon. His supper of corn bread and milk would be waiting for him. She was counting the days to my arrival date. Mama was happy and scared at the same time. She did not want to be home alone when the baby came.

It was shortly after midnight on November 5, 1936, when
Mama let out a loud scream, awaking me from my slumber

in my warm liquid blanket. I began to feel rapid movements. Mama was excited about something. The previous few months, I had become used to feeling at times that my body was spinning. Something was going on with Mama. Hours would go by when all was calm, and then suddenly my body was trembling, and I felt like I was doing somersaults. On this night, I felt my body being tightened. Mama's body was jumpy and rigid. At times when she seemed to be rushing about and trembling, I became scared. I did not know what was happening, but I felt uneasy about the frequency of the physical bumps I would feel. Mama was rushing about more than usual. At this time of night, we usually would be sleeping and it would be quiet. On this night, I heard loud noises. My body was jerking one way and then another. I was frightened by so much noise and by the movements I was feeling. I began to feel calm and sleepy. Off to the land of dreams I went. Then suddenly, I felt a pop on my behind. I let out a scream! I was angry to have been awakened. Too tired to listen to the chatter of adults, I went back to sleep.

As Mama tells this story, it was about midnight on a chilly fall night when she felt a sharp cramp-like pain in her belly. She hoped it was not time for me to make my appearance. It was pitch dark outside. The stars shone magnificently bright in the sky, but their brilliance did not light the ground. Mama shuddered at the thought of Daddy having to leave her alone while he went to get the midwife. They looked forward to the birth of their first child but had hoped the baby's arrival would be during the day.

Mama knew it would take Daddy about fifteen minutes to put the harness on Mattie and hitch her to the wagon. She thought of the long drive to and from the house of the midwife, Miss Washington, who lived near Kershaw County but was still several miles away. The round trip would take about two hours or more if Miss Washington was already attending to another birthing. In the event this was the case, it could mean hours and hours of waiting. Mama said the very thought of being alone for hours sent chills throughout her body. "It is not time for the baby to be born. It is not time for the baby to be born," she quietly kept saying over and over again. She also prayed she would not be alone when she had her first child.

Mama dreaded being left alone in Chevis Belton's old house at night. She knew that the hants never failed to appear as soon as she was alone. She began to shake as she thought of the many antics of the hants when she was alone. Mama did not want to be alone having a baby. She had to get control of herself. She got up, went to the dresser, popped two of Dr. Miles' Nervine pills into her mouth, and took two gulps of water to wash them down. She walked back slowly to the bed and eased into it gently, careful not to wake Daddy.

The pain was stronger than the previous ones. No, she could not wait any longer. She must wake Daddy immediately. He got up, pulled on his overalls, tucked in his shirt, literally jumped into his work boots while grabbing his straw hat, and headed for the stable to harness and hitch Mattie to the wagon. He checked the kerosene level in the lanterns. He lit both, put them on the side of the wagon, and got his large flashlight. He told Mama to rest, and he would be back as soon as he could.

Mama knew things would be quiet for only a little while. The hants were still as mice when cats are present, but whenever Daddy left the house, they came out from their hiding places. Within minutes, Mama would hear the rattling of pans in the kitchen. Plates would crash to the floor, and unseen items would be heard crashing against the walls.

The hants made life miserable for Mama when she was alone. She believed they knew she was afraid of them. Aunt Laura had told her to ignore them, but Mama had a hard time doing this.

When Mama heard Daddy leaving the yard, she took two more of Dr. Miles' Nervine, hoping she would go into a deep sleep and not hear the hants. With an "I don't care" attitude, she fell into a sound sleep within minutes and slept for about an hour before being awakened by a sharp pain. She looked at the clock and saw that it was 4:45 A.M. She thought Daddy should have returned by now. She wondered what was keeping him. The pain was coming faster, faster, and more intense. Mama began to panic. What would she do if he did not arrive in time with the midwife? She did not want to give birth alone.

Giving birth alone would be scary. This was her first child. She had no experience with birthing babies. Mama began to tremble. As the pains continued to come faster and more intense, she took two more of Dr. Miles' Nervine pills and told herself she had to remain calm. Mama got out of bed and began to walk around in the small bedroom. She then went into the kitchen, opened the window, and listened for the wagon. There was no sign of Daddy and the midwife. She closed the window, turned around, and saw the churn on its side in a puddle of milk. "Who did this?" she said out loud. As the last word left her mouth, she knew the hants were continuing their mischief. Mama had left the firewood stacked neatly next to the fireplace. Now the wood was scattered about. She took two more of Dr. Miles' Nervine pills. She walked slowly back to the bed and crawled into it. Mama could not sleep because of the pain. She decided to take three of Dr. Miles' Nervine pills. She began to feel groggy and peaceful and thought maybe she had taken too many Dr. Miles' Nervine pills. She knew there was not much she could do but wait.

Daddy arrived with Miss Washington, the midwife, at about 6:30 A.M. She came in and examined Mama. She told Daddy there was not much time left before the baby would arrive. Miss Washington told him to build a bigger fire in the fireplace and heat a couple of pots of water. In preparation for the birth, Mama had several clean sheets, washing cloths, little flannel blankets, and gowns. Mama had used flour sacks to make diapers, shirts, and belly bands. The baby arrived at 6:45 A.M. on November 5, 1936. The midwife cut the umbilical cord with sterilized scissors. She ripped a piece from the clean white sheet and ironed it until it was scorched. She put on a little ointment and applied it to the baby's navel. She washed and rubbed the child with baby oil, dressed her, wrapped her in a small blanket and placed her in Mama's arms.

Mama took a look at the little girl, who weighed about six pounds and had the honey tone complexion of her father. Mama checked the hair on the temples. It was fine, straight, and silky. She then checked the color of skin above the fingernail. It was almost white. *There*, she concluded that the child would definitely have her father's skin color. Mama's skin was a dark mahogany; her hair was thick and coarse. She was glad her daughter would have "good hair." It was enough to take care of her own hair, and she would not miss having to struggle with another head of hair.

The midwife asked Daddy and Mama what name they had chosen for their daughter. Both said they had not given it a thought. Indeed, they had not. Daddy had been hoping for a boy, and wanted to name him Joseph for him and his father. Mama did not want to name their firstborn Joseph. They were so busy arguing about naming their son Joseph that neither had given a thought that the baby might be a girl. Upon discovering that the young couple did not have a name for their daughter, Miss Washington offered the name Lottie. It was for Daddy's mother's sister. They accepted it and added Mae, a very popular middle name for Southern females. Mama held the baby for a few more minutes and then dropped off to sleep. It had been a long night.

Mama awakened at about 4 in the afternoon. Miss Washington made catnip tea for the baby's first feeding. Mama still felt tired, but not being one to stay put long, she got out of the bed and sat in a chair. Mama was still sitting there when Daddy came in at 5 P.M. from the field. He said he wanted to know how she was feeling. He was pleased to see her up and decided it would not be necessary to keep the midwife around. He asked Mama if she minded making his supper. She did not feel like it but said nothing. Mama had just given birth! A woman was supposed to stay in bed for at least three days. Mama slowly went to the pantry and got a cup of flour, a cup of cornmeal, a cup of buttermilk, salt, baking powder, and eggs, and mixed them together. Mama asked Daddy to get the skillet and place it on the fire logs to heat. She threw in a piece of butter. When the butter melted, she poured the corn bread mixture into the skillet, and Daddy set it atop the burning wood in the fireplace. When the bread had browned on one side, Mama asked Daddy to remove it from the fire, and she flipped it over to brown on the other side. When the bread had cooked, she cut a slice for him, poured a glass of fresh buttermilk with lots of butter on top, and placed it on the table before him.

Daddy's habit of asking Mama to prepare his meals right after the birth of each child began with Lottie Mae, and ended with their last child, Josephine. Mama resented what she considered pure selfishness on Daddy's part and likened it to treating her no better than the cows. They drop their calves and are expected to continue providing for others without skipping a beat. As the years went by, Mama also would speak often of slavery time and the slave masters who required mothers to return to the fields shortly after giving birth. Daddy's behavior was the beginning of a tropical storm in their marriage. Mama never forgave Daddy for expecting her to provide for the family following childbirth, but she never said she regretted marrying him.

CHAPTER 4 — THE COURTSHIP

Mama and Daddy met during the spring of 1935 at Mount Olive Baptist Church in Longtown, South Carolina, while attending a spring revival meeting. The weeklong revival series was popular with church members. Local churches took turns holding revival meetings in the spring and fall. It was a rivalry as to who got the best preacher, put on the best feast, and got the most new members. The youth saw the revival meetings as opportunities to find their true love and get their first kiss when the elders were looking elsewhere.

Mount Olive Baptist and Antioch Baptist Churches were located within walking distance to many families in rural Longtown. Mount Olive Baptist was at the center of Longtown, while Antioch was off the main thoroughfare to the Wateree River. Services were held at each church on alternating Sundays. Families usually chose the churches closest to them. By alternating Sundays, many families had an opportunity to attend both churches. Oftentimes, a husband would be a member of one church and the wife a member of another. Sometimes the children would choose different churches as well. Mama's parents and siblings were members of Antioch Baptist Church, and Daddy's family held membership in Mount Olive Baptist Church and Mount Joshua Methodist in Kershaw County. Church services were an important part of family life. Adults and children attended church every Sunday. There was no work on Sunday. It was the Lord's Day. Some saw Sunday as a day of rest and worship. Families would depart for church in early morning before the sun got hot. They would walk along narrow, dusty dirt roads leading to Antioch and Mount Olive Baptist Churches. Babies and small children were carried in their mother's arms or on their father's shoulders.

Mama said the happiest time of the week was going to church on Sundays. Churches filled a social need for young people to meet people. Mama and her siblings attended no parties or dances, as Grandpa Saul viewed these as sinful. She had some opportunity for social life at school, which was opened only a few months of the year, but she spent little time there because of the demands of the farm. When school let out, Mama could not dally and engage in conversation with other children. She had to rush home and perform chores before sunset. Grandpa Saul kept a clock with him at all times and took note of what time she got home. If she and her sister Scillar were even a couple of minutes late arriving from school, he asked them to give an account of what happened. Grandpa Saul would begin to fuss and would not let up until bedtime. Mama said he wanted everything done his way and by his clock. Being late coming home from school two days in a row would elicit a threat from him to use his strap. Grandpa Saul was known for his beatings, and no one in their right mind wanted a whipping from him.

Mama said she had to work especially swiftly to perform her chores and assist her sister Scillar who did everything at a snail's pace. They had to work as a team. If the work did not get done well and quickly, both she and Scillar would pay the consequences. The burden was always on Mama to get the work done. Her sister was slow because of a vision problem. Mama knew what was wrong, but her parents did not acknowledge it. Mama would lead Scillar along the path to and from school, and when the sun set, Scillar could not see at all. While doing chores, Mama had to watch out for Scillar to keep her from walking into something. The barnyard contained many large pieces of farm equipment and livestock. The mules and horses were gentle, but not if you bumped into them. There would be a major problem if one crossed the path of an aggressive bull. Mama was always on the lookout to avoid a collision with equipment or a farm animal.

After working in the fields a half day on Saturdays, Mama would spend the remainder of the day preparing for Sunday. She would fetch two large pails of water from the spring, which was a quarter of a mile from the house. She poured the water from one pail into a small black wash pot and built a fire under it. When the water reached a very warm temperature, she used a dipper to remove the water to a large pail. Mama used a bar of soap made with lye to wash her hair. Then she rinsed the suds from her hair with the other pail of water. Next she used an old fork to untangle her hair and sat in the sun for her hair to dry as she waited her turn to use the straightening comb after her sisters. Mama at times became impatient, and instead of waiting for the straightening comb, she would heat a smoothing iron and use it to get some of the kinks out of her hair. She did this by placing her long hair on the ironing board and pressing it, beginning at the nape and proceeding to the ends. She then would sweep the warm smoothing iron over her entire head. This method got more of the kinks out of her hair but did not make it straight. Mama would make two corn rows and two large braids in the back, and crisscross the braids together to create a large bun in the back and other times she would twist paper into long strips and roll her hair to make curls. At night, she tied a cloth on her head tightly to hold the hair in place. She did all of this without a mirror.

Saturday night was bathing time. Mama had to make a second trip to the spring to get water for a bath. She walked slowly to and from the spring, careful not to perspire, as she did not want her hair to "turn back." There was competition between the sisters for the large washtub. While the water was heating for the bath, Mama would choose one of two dresses to wear. She did not like wearing gloves, or carrying parasols or handbags. Mama marched to her own beat and always wore plain dresses that her mother made. For one occasion her parents bought her a dress made of rayon. Rayon dresses were popular and highly prized. The drawback of wearing it was when it rained: you never wanted to be wearing your beautiful rayon dress during a downpour because it would surly shrink. Before putting on the rayon dress, Mama would check the sky for thunderclouds. She would accessorize it with a simple piece of jewelry. One earring was often all she had. She never cared if the earring matched her dress or not. Mama said she always wore a single strand of pearls, a practice she continued until her death at age ninety-four.

Young people could hardly wait until Sunday, knowing they would have an opportunity to see that "special" person. There was never an argument about going to church early. Young people would have an opportunity to sit together or near each other during church services and Sunday school, and to talk while waiting for service to begin. At church, they had many opportunities to interact, pass a note, give a smile, or hold hands when adults were not looking. However, adults always seemed to be looking. Services lasted all day and sometimes into the evening, yet at the end of service, no one rushed home. Adults enjoyed the socializing after church. This gave young people further opportunity to continue their conversations.

The young people really liked nighttime service. They were required to stay in the church yard; however, they would stand on the edge. They obeyed their parents by standing on the edge, but the kerosene lanterns gave off only dim light, giving the young people a sense of privacy and an opportunity to hold hands. So they enjoyed the company of the opposite sex in the moonlight.

Mama caught Daddy's attention during the April revival meeting on a Sunday night. He was attracted to women with ebony skin color. "The blacker the berry, the sweeter the juice," was his mantra. Mama excited him with her deep dark skin and sweet disposition. Daddy was a handsome young man. He stood about six feet with a slim physique, honey tone complexion, and green-gray eyes, and was smooth talking. For the next few Sundays, they talked briefly with one another. Mama had been seeing a fellow named Tucker, but she was not quite sure he was the one. Grandpa Saul had very strict rules. He did not allow his daughters to entertain more than one fellow at a time. He forbade them from bringing home one fellow this Sunday and another one the following Sunday. Mama had to make sure she was willing to discontinue the relationship with Tucker. She needed to be certain that Daddy was as interested in her as she was in him. So began the dance.

Mama and Daddy lived several miles apart and saw each other only on Sunday. There was no other way of communicating. Sending a letter required walking to the mailbox more than a mile away. She had no stamps and no time to go to a mailbox. Grandpa Saul would not have allowed her to take time away from farm work. Grandpa Saul tried to watch their every movement. When Daddy asked to walk Mama home after church, she agreed.

When a guy is really interested, he shows this by asking permission to walk you home. The first time Daddy walked Mama home Grandpa Saul was a little concerned. "Here we go again with a new guy," he bellowed. The following Sunday, Daddy walked Mama halfway home and asked to be excused. He said he had an errand to do for his father. He did the same thing the next Sunday. On the third Sunday, as they were strolling down the road, he told Mama he had to turn back. She let him know she was fully aware of what he was doing. He was not doing errands for his father, but was racing back to catch up with Rachel to walk her home and spend time with her. Mama was not going to play second to anyone. She told Daddy he had a choice: walk her all the way home or just walk out of her life. This was probably the first time Daddy had encountered a woman who challenged him and gave him options that he had to choose on the spot. Daddy learned that Mama was very sweet but more than a handful when she got angry. He liked the feisty Mama even more and continued walking until they reached the Stones' farm.

Occasionally, Mama had to go fetch water from the spring, and Daddy would walk with her. Grandpa Saul sent the three youngest brothers, McKinley, Boykin, and Prince, along to keep an eye on the couple. Mama would become enraged. As soon as she was out of Grandpa Saul's sight, she and Daddy would run to the spring, leaving the little brothers far behind and unable to watch their every move. They used this time to kiss. Mama would intimidate her brothers by threatening that if they told Grandpa Saul they could not watch her every move because she ran and left them behind, she would beat them up. She said that was enough to keep their little mouths shut.

Courtship was not easy. Mama's father kept a close eye on his daughters, and the fellows. When the couples sat in the sitting room, he would always be in the next room with an ear to the door. When the clock struck 9 P.M., he would clear his throat very loudly. If that did not work instantaneously, he would turn over a chair, causing it to make a loud crashing sound as it hit the floor. A minute later, he would say loudly, "It's 9 o'clock. It is time for people to go to bed. Everyone should be home by now, or getting ready to go home." With that remark, the fellow would say, "I am going home. See you next Sunday."

The couple would proceed to the door, walking slowly, of course, and dallying a minute to say goodbyes. While Grandpa Saul could not see the couple, he listened carefully for every movement. If the goodbyes took too long, he yelled from his room, "What's going on out there? I heard the fellow say he was leaving. How long does it take to walk to the door? He should have been halfway home by now." Of course, this was an exaggeration as the fellow lived many miles away.

The courting couples had no privacy. While Grandpa Saul could only listen to what was being said, he sent Mama's three younger brothers to peek through the window shutters and watch the couple. Mama was very annoyed by this surveillance. She thought this spying was uncalled for and that anyone with a bit of sense should know that courting couples would want to kiss once in a while. But Mama kept these thoughts to herself. According to Mama, Grandpa Saul did not allow anyone, including Grandma Ella, to talk back to him or express an opinion that differed from his.

With the hard farm work of plowing and harvesting the crops, and the lack of freedom to attend even a ball game, Mama longed for an opportunity to escape from what she called "prison." When Daddy asked for her hand in marriage, she viewed it as an escape to freedom. For Mama, there was no hell like living under the roof of Solomon Stone.

Chapter 5 — The Wedding

With the wedding date set for November 28, 1935, it was time to begin preparations for that special day. So Grandma Ella and Mama asked their neighbor, Mr. Boykin, if they could hitch a ride to Winnsboro on his next trip there. They knew it would be an all-day trip, as Mr. Boykin took care of business, and visited relatives and friends while there. This was just fine with them. They would not need to hurry to shop and they could have a late visit with Grandma's sister Sarah, whose nickname was Miss Sweet Mouth, and her husband Ben, who was Grandpa Saul's brother. They left early morning and returned just before sundown.

For the next two weeks, Grandma Ella was busy preparing for the wedding. She was eager to make the dress and get that out of the way, as there was so much work to be done and not a lot of time. In addition to preparing for the wedding and performing other household duties for her large family, she had a demanding husband. The next morning, following the trip to Winnsboro, Grandma Ella arose very early and gathered an old sheet to use in making the dress pattern. She also found an old dress of hers, which would be very helpful in making a pattern for the sleeves and collar. Grandma Ella and Mama had decided on a full skirt, with gathers at the waist. The bodice would be the most difficult to make, as they wanted to insert the lace in the front of the bodice. The dress would have long sleeves. During the week, Grandma Ella worked on the dress in the early mornings and late into the evenings. At the end of the week, she had created a beautiful wedding dress for Mama. When Mama tried on the dress for the final fitting, Grandma Ella admired her beautiful daughter looking regal in a dress of her creation. The eggshell color of the dress contrasted with Mama's ebony skin color. Grandma Ella recalled the days of her youth when she too was slim and gorgeous. She was still a beautiful woman, but she had added many pounds, and looked tired and weary—older than her years. Living with Solomon Stone had not been easy for her or the children. He was a hard man. As she admired her daughter, she prayed life would be easier for her.

With the dress completed, Grandma Ella turned her attention to the planning and preparation of the food. She wanted to have plenty of food. No one was going to say that Ella Stone had a skimpy dinner for her daughter's wedding. So she went to the chicken coop and chose the two largest turkeys and five chickens. She selected two cured hams from the smokehouse. Then she asked Grandpa Saul if he would butcher a small calf for the wedding. He agreed. However, when he learned of the turkeys, chickens, and hams, he asked Grandma Ella if she was expecting an army. He thought she was going overboard. According to Mama, this was the first wedding of a daughter. Other daughters just ran off, got married, and then made the announcement. As Grandpa observed the amount of time taken to prepare for the wedding dinner, he commented that he did not understand why: "Stell did not run away and get married like her sisters." Grandpa Saul was not a sentimental man. He was all work at home and at church.

The day of the wedding was a balmy fall day. The sun shone brightly, and the garden still had beautiful blooming flowers. Daddy arranged to pick up Mama and her parents. He had borrowed his father's Model T Ford. They traveled to Winnsboro, to a justice of the peace who performed the ceremony. They arrived at about 10 A.M. but had to wait about two hours. Mama said that white people did not move quickly for black people. They made you wait even if there was no reason. It was the power they had, and they seized every opportunity to use it. Of course, the justice of the peace and his assistant probably took note of the wedding party's dress, and especially Solomon Stone. While they were working class, they were well dressed. Solomon Stone was a very proud man who walked with his chest stuck out and his head held high at all times. This practice of his always annoyed whites especially those who did not know him. It was suspected the waiting had nothing to do with the time of the justice of the peace, but everything to do with the skin color and dress of the people seeking his service.

When the justice of the peace announced the couple husband and wife, Mama said it was the sweetest moment for her. It was true she loved her husband, but it was also true she felt a great relief—"Freedom, freedom!"

The wedding party returned to the bride's home to a waiting crowed of relatives, neighbors, and friends. The tables were set. Her sisters, Lela, Janie, Rosa, and Laura, had arranged everything in accordance with their mother's instructions.

The guests included Daddy's father, Joe, and his common-law wife, Julia. It also included all of Daddy's brothers and sisters, along with their wives and husbands, and Mama's brothers and sisters. Uncles and aunts of the couple attended, along with their spouses and children. Neighbors, including the Butler and Tucker families, attended as well.

Grandpa Joe walked with a limp and was often seen wearing overalls and a felt hat—never a suit—but was dressed for the occasion. Grandpa Joe was not happy about his son's choice of marriage to Mama. When he learned of the proposal, he was overheard saying, "I did not expect Possey [Daddy's nickname] to marry a gal that was so black." Mama was quick to take offense to his comment and noted that Julia was blacker than she.

Grandpa Saul blessed the tables of food, the newlyweds, and all who had gathered. The spread of food was something to behold. The guests had many choices: roast turkey with corn bread dressing, fried chicken smothered in brown gravy, stew beef, roast beef, baked ham, baked macaroni and cheese, cabbage, rutabaga, turnips, fried corn, and lima beans. The dessert table held coconut cake, chocolate cake, apple pies, and sweet potato pies. The wedding cake was a seven-layer yellow cake with plum jelly filling and white frosting. The comments were that the wedding cake, courthouse style, was the best Ella Stone had made. Mama said she never tasted a cake so delicious, and no one is known to top Grandma Ella's cake.

As the sun began to set, Mama and Daddy departed with his father and Cuzin Julia. The young couple would stay with them until they could find a house of their own.

Over the years, Mama would describe the courtship between her and Daddy and the preparations for the wedding by Grandma Ella. It was a special occasion for her, filled with sweet memories. Through her eighty-fourth birthday, she spoke fondly of the event as though it had happened yesterday, recalling in detail the wedding, the dress, and the cake.

CHAPTER 6 — FREDDIE - 1938

When Mama and Daddy moved to the new house Grandpa Joe built for them, they carried with them a mule, a cow, a bull, a dog, a cat, a pig, and a couple of chickens. The move was perfect timing. Mama had been unhappy when Daddy had to work far away, but now she would be close to Cuzin Julia, and Daddy would be nearby as he assisted his daddy, Grandpa Joe, with farm work. In addition, he had to work his own plot of land that Grandpa Joe had allocated to him. Mama and Daddy partitioned the large room to have separate sleeping and cooking areas. The new house was ready for occupancy in time for Freddie's birth late in the afternoon on January 2, 1938. According to Mama, he was a very small baby with a reddish complexion, the same as Daddy.

Freddie was an active baby and kept Mama busy thinking of ways to contain him in one spot. A makeshift playpen would soon become a bed of rubble. Mama would make a tent to keep the scorching sun off Freddie, but within minutes he had the tent down. He managed to tangle himself in the materials and then would scream for her. She had to stop her work to untangle him.

The sun was not the only enemy of a small child. Mammoth red ants loved the taste of babies' young, tender skin. Mama was very resourceful and used breadcrumbs to lure the ants away from Freddie while she worked in the field. Freddie, the explorer, found the crumbs and ate them. The red ants found him and began to feast on him. Again, Mama stopped work and rushed to him.

During the first year of his life, Freddie became so ill Mama and Daddy thought they would lose him. He became listless and would not eat. Mama rubbed him down with oils and salves. There was no improvement. Getting to a doctor was not easy, and money was needed, which they did not have. They took turns rocking Freddie. In desperation, not knowing what else could be done, Mama decided to give Freddie a spoonful of water. Surprisingly, he greedily sucked it all up. She kept feeding him water until he wanted no more. Mama said Freddie perked up like a withered plant that had been deprived of water and was dying. From that day on, Mama said, she made sure all her children drank plenty of water. This was a practice she continued with family members through the generations. If a child was not feeling well, Mama would inquire of the parent, "When was the last time you gave that child some water?"

Mama said Freddie walked at seven months, earlier than the other children. Freddie said he began working sooner than the other children and had worked for as long as he could remember. On the farm, small children were taught early to fetch a pail or dipper of water, and to tote small items to parents. Children were observed as to their physical strength and mental alertness. This helped parents decide their readiness to join others in the fields. While Mama was busy working and keeping an eye on Freddie, I became ill. Mama and Daddy stayed up all night rocking me and rubbing my chest with oils. A doctor later determined that I had double pneumonia. This was another scare for them.

No one knows when or why Freddie got the nickname Buddy Boy. In Longtown, there were nicknames such as Buddy Roll, Buddy, Little Buddy, and Big Buddy. The nicknames stuck like glue. Freddie became forever known as Buddy Boy until he moved to Connecticut in 1956. There he was called Freddie. However, in Longtown, South Carolina, he is still known as Buddy Boy.

CHAPTER 7 — SOLOMON - 1939

The third child, Solomon Wesley Bell, was born on March 17, 1939, and named for his maternal grandfather, Solomon Stone. He was given the nickname Saul, the same as his grandfather. People born in March were viewed as changeable as the weather in March. One day it is sunny and calm, the next day cloudy and windy, and the next day after that may find the weather snowy or freezing. March was a frustrating time for farmers in Longtown. Just when they felt confident that spring had arrived and it was safe to plant, the weather would return to wintry conditions, destroying the freshly planted fields. If you were born in March, you were branded for life as unpredictable, subject to an irritable disposition one day and a very pleasant one the next. You learned early on as a child to beware of anyone who was born in March.

As a child, Saul took on the personality of March. You never knew if the day with him was going to be sunny or if fierce cold wind would engulf you. He lived up to March the calm and March the furor. He was born in the evening. The exact time is not known. What is known is that upon his arrival, Saul grabbed Daddy in the collar and held him. Daddy was indeed surprised. He commented on the strong grip of his newborn son. Mama said she recognized that grip as a sign her third child would be a fighter.

Solomon Grundy,
Born on a Monday,
Christened on Tuesday,
Married on Wednesday,
Took ill on Thursday,
Grew worse on Friday,
Died on Saturday,
Buried on Sunday.
That was the end
Of Solomon Grundy.
                    — James Orchard Halliwell, published 1842

Saul received the nickname of Solomon Grundy from schoolchildren who regularly teased him by chanting this rhyme. Of course, the children took care to remain at a distance when they taunted him, as the nickname would elicit a fistfight. Saul was always ready with his south-paw to execute unforgettable blows upon his tormentors when he found them within reach. He would lie in wait for them. It was not long before his cousins and others learned not to mess with "Solomon Grundy." Saul's motto was, "If I don't get you now, I will get you later." He was true to his word.

Saul proclaimed he was the baby although he was the third of eight children. The baby holds a special place in a family, as did "King Solomon," as he became affectionately known, when there was jockeying among siblings for a favorable position. He always felt he was special.

During his early years, Saul joined his brother Freddie and his cousins in many activities, including swimming in the creek. Toys were very few because parents could not afford them. So Saul and his play companions found a variety of ways to entertain themselves, such as chasing chickens and killing them for Sunday dinner, killing water moccasins and other snakes for fun, tearing down wasps' nests with bare hands, and making boxes to trap rabbits and doing "surgery" on their hind legs by cutting a ligament. This was a method devised by the boys who they claimed did not hurt the rabbit, but made it so it could only hop instead of run. This allowed the boys to play with the rabbit until near dinnertime when they would present their catch to their parents, who would kill the rabbit, skin it, wash it, and prepare it for dinner. Within about forty-five minutes, the family would sit down to enjoy fried rabbit smothered in brown gravy, and onions over white rice. There would be fresh baked corn bread and churned buttermilk. The next day the boys would be on the lookout for another plaything.

One day Saul was alone when he caught a rabbit. He was excited and decided this was an opportunity to perform "surgery" on the rabbit's back legs just the way he had witnessed the procedure done by the older boys. Saul decided he would have it as a plaything before presenting it to Mama for dinner. Believing he was following the instructions correctly, he skinned the rabbit's back legs and made an incision. When he placed the rabbit on the ground, it ran at lightning speed into the woods. Saul was shocked. He stood speechless as he watched the rabbit find safety in the woods. Saul went home disappointed and empty-handed.

CHAPTER 8 — DAVID, 1940

On July 9, 1940, David, the fourth child, arrived. It was said that he was a belated birthday gift for Mama, as her birthday was on July 2. There was no fanfare about David's birth. Mama had become accustomed to childbirth. Also, David's birth was indeed at a very convenient time. The crops had been "laid by." There was no further plowing of the crops. It was July, and it was a time to celebrate the Fourth of July with firecrackers, picnics, eating newly ripened watermelons, roasting and boiling the first crop of sweet corn, and making the delicious okra, tomato, and corn soups to be eaten with a large piece of freshly baked corn bread made with lots of country butter and freshly churned buttermilk. Summertime was always good because there was plenty to eat and the pace had slowed. There was time for fishing. Saturday night fish fry was popular and mostly held in homes.

By the time of David's birth, Mama had developed excellent organizational skills. She took steps to ensure that her workload would be light for several days after giving birth. Some women took a couple of weeks off from day work, but that did not apply to Mama. She had three small children and a husband who demanded her attention. In preparation for the baby's arrival, Mama washed and ironed sufficient clothes for the family's use during her short convalescent period. She made sure the yard was swept daily. She washed, straightened, and braided her hair and mine. She prepared enough food for a few days.

Mama said David made his appearance quickly after a few sharp pains. One look at him and Mama saw that he had deep ebony skin color, the same as she and Saul. Freddie and I had Daddy's honey skin color. Of course, Mama had no color preference when it came to her children. She loved them all. However, she was painfully aware of skin color prejudices, as she had experienced them growing up. Mama told me Grandpa Saul never called her by her name. It was always, "Come here, Black Gal," and "Do this, Black Gal." So Mama knew there was a real possibility that David and Saul would come face-to-face with skin color prejudices. She was not prepared for such prejudices from within her own household, however. Daddy was very unhappy about the color of his two dark-skinned sons. After a couple of years, he began relentless verbal attacks upon them that included denial of fatherhood. This created tension in our house, as Mama was forever in verbal confrontation with Daddy about his abuse of the two boys. It was not long before the verbal attacks between Mama and Daddy became physical. This created long-lasting pain for Saul and David. During stressful moments in adulthood, they would shed tears as they recalled Daddy's abusive words. Daddy did not physically abuse them because Mama did the whipping. She believed that men should not whip children, because they were strong and did not have the tender love of a mother.

As usual, Mama was up and about shortly after David's birth. There was no time to sit idle. David not only shared Mama's skin coloring, but also suffered from asthma, the same as she. Medical care was not affordable and not easily accessible. When David suffered from asthmatic symptoms, it was necessary at times for Mama to walk, carrying David, several miles to get medical help. Mama used a variety of home remedies, including horehound tea, to try easing David's symptoms.

Horehound tea was used for everything that ailed you, a practice Mama learned from Grandpa Saul. She also marked David's height on the wall. It was said that when the child grew beyond the mark, he or she would be cured of asthma. It did not work for David. He joined Freddie, Saul, and me in Mama's day-to-day life.

CHAPTER 9 — MACARTHUR, 1942

Two years later, on July 8, 1942, another brother made his appearance in this world with little fanfare. Babies were born all the time in Long-town. There were now four brothers: Freddie, Saul, David, and MacArthur. I was hoping for a sister. I was just sick and tired of the boys, but they seemed to keep coming. With MacArthur, David, and Mama sharing birthdays in July, and so close, there was no way of forgetting either of their birthdays. There was always a celebration.

Each time a baby boy was born, Daddy would beg Mama to name their son Joe for him and his father. Mama would always refuse. MacArthur's birth was no different. Daddy would plead, and Mama would refuse. There was a deadlock. This time, however, Mama had an unlikely ally in Grandpa Joe. Mama and Grandpa Joe disliked each other intensely and did not get along. Mama believed it was because of her dark skin color. She was still fuming over his remark that he did not think Daddy would choose someone "so black." Mama would not forgive him for this. Also adding to the "stew pot" was Mama's sharp tongue. She talked back to Grandpa Joe, which no one else did. But on the birth of the fourth son, Mama and Grandpa Joe agreed on naming their new child for World War II General Douglas MacArthur. Grandpa Joe admired General MacArthur and thought him to be the greatest general of all time.

We lived in the flight path of military planes and could hear them in the distance as they roared forward. Grandpa Joe would stop whatever he was doing and wait for their arrival overhead. He would get excited, take off his old brown felt hat with holes, and began waving as soon as the planes glided over the treetops. He would jump up and down, and run to follow the planes as they flew by. Grandpa Joe would shout messages to General MacArthur, telling him what a good job he was doing. He would keep up his performance until the planes were out of sight and he was out of breath. By then he needed a rest. Everyone joined him for a few minutes of rest. Occasionally, Grandpa Joe would give Hitler salutes and do the goose strut. Never understood why he did this. However, everyone enjoyed the break from work.

MacArthur was born with skin as white as any white baby. You just could not tell the difference. The old women would check the color around his fingernails. This was supposed to tell what color he would eventually be. They could not figure this out with MacArthur. There was a lot of guessing. MacArthur was taken to the fields along with the rest of the children. Mama placed him on a blanket under a shade tree. Saul, Freddie, and I did whatever little hands could do. David was still too small to do any work.

As MacArthur grew, he became quite aware of his skin color. He began to compare his color with that of Bobby, whose paternal grandfather was white, and Willie and Charles, whose father was white. If they were white, MacArthur reasoned he was certainly white as well, as his skin color was the same as theirs. Skin color was a real issue. It seemed to define who you are, and whether you were good or bad.

MacArthur learned early of the benefits of having "white" skin. On New Year's Day, MacArthur was chosen to be the official first visitor at Miss Red's house. Her son, Bobby, was the first visitor at our house. They received gifts for their visits. This was a ritual that was practiced for many years. No one else dared to show their faces at either house before MacArthur's and Bobby's visits. It was believed that if someone with dark skin or a female was your first visit, you would be in for bad luck for the year. It was often said, "The lighter the skin of the first visitor, the brighter your future."

As the years went by, MacArthur's skin did a slow color change, similar to leaves in the fall. It gradually changed from white to rosy red, then yellow, and finally a light bronze, a color most white folks would die to have during the summer months. He did not weep over this change, but joined in the laughter as he was teased.

Uncle George, Daddy's brother, had an identity problem of his own before MacArthur was born. He declared that he was Indian and not black. When asked how he could be Indian when his father, mother, sisters, and brothers were black, Uncle George would point to his straight, silky hair and his light burnt bronze colored skin as evidence. He would cry like a baby when no one seemed to believe him. MacArthur, on the other hand, did not care what anyone thought. Looking back sixty-plus years later, Uncle George may have been correct that the family is of mixed blood, as evidenced by our fair skin and silky hair. On Mama's side of the family, Grandpa Saul refused to discuss any possible race mixing. He would remind inquirers that one drop of black blood made us colored regardless of how white the skin.

I recall a time that several white people showed up at Antioch Baptist Church. I had overheard adult whispers about slavery time when white people came to black churches to spy on black folks. I was frightened. However, when the church service ended, white and black people rushed toward each other with outstretched arms and embraced one another. I remember Mama introducing me to the people, saying, "This here is your people." The hugs and praises were plentiful. The hugs were tight squeezes that you remembered.

CHAPTER 10 — MOUNT OLIVE SCHOOL

Mount Olive School, a one-room, wooden frame building, was located in Longtown near the crossroad of Mount Olive Baptist Church and along the route to the Wateree River, a popular fishing site. It sat surrounded by property owners Matterson, Tuckers, Reeves, and our Grandpa Joe. Miss Maggie Derry is believed to be the first and only teacher who taught at the school, which closed in the late 1950s.

Miss Maggie Derry's skin color was dark chocolate, and her long, black hair was sprinkled with gray streaks. She had a slim figure and gold crowns on two front teeth. She wore long dresses and high-heel shoes, and she always carried an umbrella, as she walked several miles to school every day regardless of the weather. Meanwhile, a school bus passed her every morning and afternoon en route to pick up and deliver one or two white children to their school, which was a daily forty-eight-mile round trip.

Upon arrival at school in the morning, Miss Maggie Derry would build a fire in the large, black potbelly stove. Children living nearby would watch for the chimney smoke before leaving for school. About fifty students were in attendance during the school year.

Miss Maggie Derry began school with all students standing and reciting the Pledge of Allegiance, the Lord's Prayer, and lastly, the school's motto: "Do unto others as you would have them do unto you. Give to the world the best you have and the best will come back to you." The motto was written in large lettering across the top of the blackboard as a reminder.

Miss Maggie Derry taught first through eighth grades. Some students did not have her attention until near the end of the day. While waiting, the students were not to talk, fall asleep, or create any disturbance. You listened and waited patiently for your turn. Children were told to use the outhouse during recess so there would be no interruptions. Our school did not have electricity. On cloudy days, it was difficult to read.

Miss Maggie Derry had no natural children, but helped raised two nephews, Ben and Freddie, who came to school along with her. Freddie was older than the other children and devilish. He would control the heating of the stove. The younger and smaller children would get pushed to the back of the room where there was little heat. I complained about his behavior to Miss Maggie Derry, who declared that everyone had to take a turn near the heating stove. Freddie got very angry. When it came my turn to be close to the stove, Freddie piled more wood into it. When I got warmed and was ready to return to my seat, he blocked me and made me sit longer, watching while I roasted.

Parents provided loads of wood to the school to help keep it warn. At times it was necessary for the older boys to leave school in search of additional wood to heat the school. Permission was always sought from landowners before going on their property.

Our school was given discarded books from the white schools. Some pages were missing and many others were covered with scribbles. Used desks given to us were damaged, with many carvings in them. However, Miss Maggie Derry was happy to receive the books and furniture for her students.

I still recall with humor the first visit of Miss Dove, the white school nurse. She was visibly shocked when she saw the room filled with about fifty children. About a third were very dark-skinned; another third were blond, blue-eyed, and fair-skinned. Then there were the honey skin tones with long, straight hair. As Miss Dove stood in the doorway seemingly unable to move or speak, Miss Maggie Derry cheerfully, with a smile, said to her, "Come in. Come in. Welcome! Welcome to my beautiful flower garden." We noted that when Miss Dove spoke to our teacher, she called her Maggie.

A few years after Miss Dove's visit, my sister Alberta, who had just started school, stood up and announced to all that she had a boyfriend. Miss Maggie Derry was shocked that someone so young had a boyfriend. She was curious, as were the other children, so she asked Alberta who her boyfriend was. With the biggest smile, Alberta pointed at Charles, saying, "The little white boy with the blond hair and blue eyes." The children roared with laughter. Miss Maggie Derry tried to contain herself but was unsuccessful.

Miss Maggie Derry was the widow of Reverend Eli Derry, brother of Janie Derry, who was the mother of our grandfather Solomon Stone. Reverend Eli Derry and Miss Maggie Derry were active members of Antioch Baptist Church. She taught Sunday school there, along with Grandpa Saul, for many years. She presented children's programs for Easter Sunday, Mother's Day, Children's Day, and Father's Day. The programs provided opportunities for the children to sing, recite, and participate in presentations. On Easter Sunday, most children would choose the Bible verse "Jesus wept." They stepped on the stage, dressed in their Sunday best, and said, "Jesus wept," with poise. Each child spoke the two words in their own style. Some said it loudly, others softly. Some ended with a slow, deep bow, and others spoke the words rapidly, running off the stage at the same time. Regardless of how the speaking was done, each child received generous applause and much praise as they left the stage. There were more words of praise and encouragement following the service.

The tradition of children's participation remains to this day. Seventy years later, I enjoyed listening to my cousin Beno recite speeches such as, "Roses on my shoulders, slippers on my feet. I am my mommy's baby, and don't you think I am sweet?" and "Why are you looking at me? I did not come here to stay. I come to wish you Happy Easter." Children were encouraged to memorize their speech. "Jesus loves me, this I know, for the Bible tells me so." If a child forgot their line, they still got loud applause. Children were always encouraged and praised for their participation.

Many of the dark-skinned children thought Miss Maggie showed preference for children whose father or grandfather was white, but I could not say this was true based on my experience. Miss Maggie Derry was proud of her students and demanded that everyone be on their good behavior in school and church. She sought to bring out the best you had to offer. She told us the story of Will and Can't: Can't said he could not climb the hill and did not. Will said, "I can and will climb the hill," and he did. We were urged to never say "can't."

Miss Maggie Derry was stern and dedicated, and instilled in her students a desire to learn and a respect for themselves and others. Some still recall the crack of her long-reaching switch on their hand. Others repeat the school motto as a reminder to "give to the world the best you have and the best will come back to you." Miss Maggie Derry is fondly remembered by her students.

CHAPTER 11 — FARM LIFE

Mama said farm life required your attention from sunup to sundown and from January to January. One cycle would end, and another cycle began. In January, Daddy and Mama began to knock down cotton stalks and remove them from the field. Come February, the ground had to be plowed and turned over in preparation for seeding. In early March, the farmers began to spread fertilizer and plant seeds. The weather was not always cooperative in early spring, especially March. There was a schedule for planting cotton and all produce. Next came weeding and tilling the fields to have a large and healthy crop. In August, revival meetings began and usually were held Monday through Sunday. Come September, it was time to check on the cotton's readiness for picking and get the corn ready for grinding into cornmeal. Along about December, it was time for hog killing and curing meat. There was the planting time, the growing cycle, and protecting the farm from a variety of bugs and other intruders, especially boll weevils.

When time permitted between preparation and planting, folks would grab their fishing poles, baits, and hooks, and head for the Wateree Pond where the fish were always plentiful. White perch, catfish, eels, and carp were favorites. Good catches provided food for the table during the lean early springtime period before the vegetables matured.

It was always a competition. Who caught the most? Who landed the largest fish? Who had to struggle to pull in a big one without being pulled into the river? Saul and Freddie never stopped reminding me that I caught only one fish in my life but that it got away while nearly pulling me into the river. One could not afford to fall into the river since no one knew how to swim.

As the small plants began to grow, they required a daily vigil to protect them from a variety of intruders. The greatest threat to the cotton crop was the boll weevil. Mama and Daddy joined our neighbors in trying to protect their young plants from the boll weevil because it could do a lot of damage overnight. If you lose your battle with the boll weevil, you can lose your shirt, pants, and shoes! Nothing left but a "bare" behind.

A number of artists described the battle between farmers and the boll weevil in song. Many farmers' hearts rejoiced at fighting the enemy and listening to songs such as "The Boll Weevil Song" by Lead Belly. One version went like this:

> Well, the boll weevil and the little black bug
> Come from a-Mexico, they say.
> Came all the way to Texas
> Just a-lookin' for a place to stay.
> Just a-lookin' for a home, just a-lookin' for a home.
> Well, the first time that I seen the boll weevil
> He was a-sittin' on the square.
> Well, the next time that I seen him
> He had his a-family there.
> Just a-lookin' for a home, just a-lookin' for a home.
> Well, the farmer took the boll weevil,

And he put him on the red hot sand.
Well, the weevil said, this is a-mighty hot,
But I take it like a man.
This will be my home, this will be my home.
Well, the farmer took the boll weevil,
And he put him on a keg of ice.
Well, the weevil said to the farmer,
This is mighty cool and nice.
This will be my home, this will be my home.
Well, if anybody should ask you
Who it was who sang this song,
Say a guitar picker from a-Oklahoma city
With a pair of blue jeans on.
Just a-lookin' for a home, just a-lookin' for a home.

Every farmer wanted to have watermelons and corn by the Fourth of July. It was a contest who would have the first corn or watermelon. Then it became bragging time. Who grew the largest and sweetest watermelon?

Watermelons were placed in the branch to cool. At our house, we could never get enough of watermelon. When Mama and Daddy were not looking, we would hide a few for our eating pleasure, but over time, we would be found out. There was no outhouse. You did not venture off your property on to a neighbor's to "do your business." You did not go too far from the house, as you may attract a neighbor's angry dog, a wild animal, or a snake, so you "did it" near your own house. Each person had their spot. When the dogs seemingly began to enjoy "shit," Mama and Daddy would suspect something was up and investigate. If the red streaks were not blood, they were watermelon fiber. Do not try to lie!

Whipping a child for misbehaving was common practice. No child wants a whipping. Switches were made from small branches of sweet gum or peach trees. Your parents sent you to get the switch you were to be beaten with. Nothing makes a parent angrier than your returning with a small switch. The choices were that you would be beaten over-time with it or you would be sent back to get something bigger. Either way, you were in trouble. Mama did the whipping at our house. I was the only one known to be whipped by Daddy.

Farm life was not easy. Wood had to be gathered to cook food, warm water for washing clothes and dishes, and provide heat in the winter. The cows had to be milked and fed, and the women or girls of the house had to churn the milk. It was necessary to rise at the crack of dawn to get chores done before going to school or beginning the work in the field.

Chores included slopping the hogs and mopping the young cotton plants to kill the boll weevils. You mopped each plant with a mixture of molasses and arsenic, or DDT. One had to dress for the occasion with face covered, only eyes showing.

Milking was done in the early morning and before sundown. Milking a cow is easy, but the cow can be temperamental. If you are new to the task, she will be wary and turn her head to check you out. If you squeeze too hard, she may kick at you and spill the almost filled bucket of milk. Then you are in trouble. Even if you are gentle in your milking, you cannot keep trying to get as much as you can. You have to know when there is little or no milk left, or when the cow has given you as much as she wants to. If you disagree and pursue getting more from her, she will kick over the bucket and kick you also. Everyone may get a half cup of milk instead of a full cup. Fresh cooked vegetables with hot corn bread made with fresh milk and butter washed down with cold buttermilk was indescribably delicious.

The boys and men would take the mules and cows to the branch nightly for water. The chickens had to be fed. Even a small child could throw corn to the chickens.

Freddie, David, Saul, and Cousin Sammie Lee joined Daddy or Uncle George on nighttime hunting trips for coon and possum. They took along shotguns and dogs. Sometimes, after chasing their prey up and down hills, they would lose their way. On clear nights, they would wait for the stars to guide them back home. On cloudy nights, they had to wait until morning. Successful hunts in winter meant meat on the table. Rabbits and other wild animals were delicious when fried and smothered with gravy. Freddie helped to catch rabbits for the table. He began at an early age trapping rabbits in boxes. He would get up early in the morning to collect his catch.

Mama was Daddy's helpmate. She had learned farming under the stern guidance of her father. She joined Daddy and took long, heavy wooden handles, about an inch in diameter, to knock down cotton stalks and clear the field. As the weather turned warmer in early spring, Mama sowed fertilizer without gloves, which made her hands peel.

To do field work, women wore long dresses and long-sleeve cotton shirts that helped prevent scratches and rashes from plants. They covered their heads with wide-brim straw hats and wrapped cotton cloths around their foreheads with gypsum leaves to help catch the sweat and keep their bodies cool. Gypsum weed was good for headaches as well.

On the farm, all hands were at work. As soon as a child could walk without falling down, he or she was expected to help out, even if it was just fetching a dipper of water, bringing an adult their shoes, throwing corn to the chickens, going to the spring to fetch a bucket of water, churning the milk, or fanning flies away from the food. Old folks could always find something for the smallest child to do, and they always did.

Chapter 12 — Becoming A Church Member

Baptism is a special family and religious event at churches in Longtown. To become a church member, one must first accept the invitation extended by the minister when he opens the door of the church. He extends the invitation to anyone who wishes to become a church member and is ready to accept Jesus Christ as his or her Lord and Savior. At about the age of twelve, it is expected that a young person who has been brought up in the church is ready to make this commitment. Chairs are placed in the front of the pulpit with a deacon on each side. Individuals who are ready to accept the invitation simply walk up front and sit in a chair. At the end of the invitational call, the minister will ask a prospective candidate a few questions, including his or her readiness and willingness to do God's work. He or she will be asked directly if he or she accepts Jesus Christ as his or her Lord and Savior. By answering yes, the person will be accepted as a candidate. This begins the process for baptism and becoming a member of the church.

The candidate must consent to baptism by full immersion. It is an occasion that requires special preparation. Candidates are dressed in white. Females wear long, white dresses with undergarments and wrap their heads turban style with a white cloth. Males wear white pants and shirts.

Churches that do not have a pool inside the church arrange to have the baptism in an open, outside pool of water that has been cleaned and determined safe for baptism. Antioch Baptist Church chose a pool of water located down the hill across from the church. The candidates and members of the congregation would form a single line and walk along a rocky path to the pool, which was surrounded by trees and bushes. The pastor would lead the way, followed by the candidates, and the choir clapping and singing, "Going to the river to be baptized."

The preacher takes his position in the water. As each candidate approaches the pool to be baptized, the choir begins singing, "Wade in the Water Chillun" Then each candidate takes their step into the water and proceeds to meet the minister. This is a solemn moment. The minister says to the candidate, "You join the church to be baptized in the name of the Father, Son, and Holy Ghost." The candidate answers, "Yes." Then the minister presses the candidate backward until there is full immersion. The church mother leaders are ready with several white sheets to wrap each person as they leave the water. Particular care is taken to fully cover the bodies of the women and girls.

After all candidates have been baptized, the minister, followed by the candidates and the choir, return to the church singing, "I have been baptized." After being dried and dressed, the candidates sit in the front of the church to receive the right hand of fellowship from the minister, the deacons, and the members of the congregation.

After the baptism, the church ladies would arrange outside tables with lots of food. It is a day of celebration, the beginning of a new life for new members, and a day of remembrance for all.

Chapter 13 — Retreats At Grandparents' House

As far back as I can remember, our house was very turbulent. Daddy was quick to accuse Mama of infidelity if she exchanged a simple greeting with a man taking a shortcut by our house on the way to Kershaw County or a nearby neighbor. If Mama hummed or sang along with a romantic song on the radio, Daddy would accuse her of making plans to meet "her man." If a piece of straw, pine needle, or dry leaf was seen in her hair, this was evidence she was sleeping around. This pushed Mama over the edge. With her razor-sharp tongue, Mama told Daddy he was crazy. Then the beatings began. Mama was no match against Daddy's strength. Rather than stay and be beaten, Mama would run toward the home of Grandpa Joe and Cuzin Julia, who stood at the edge of the creek and urged Mama on, yelling, "Run, Stell, run! Run, Stell, run!" When Mama reached Cuzin Julia, Daddy stopped in his tracks. After a few fights, I began to cry nonstop, saying I wanted to run away. The only place to run to was the home of my grandparents Solomon and Ella Stone.

Mama and Daddy would drive me miles to my grandparents, sometimes in the middle of the night. During the visit, I was treated like company and slept in the nicest bedroom all alone. Grandma Ella made breakfast, pulling special preserves from the kitchen pantry. I felt special and enjoyed being the princess for a few days. No work. Just curl up in a soft, beautiful bed with starched sheets and a beautiful bedspread. I had my own room. It was truly a retreat.

It also was a time to talk with Grandma Ella. She told the story of mistaking two of her grandchildren for "half-white" babies. As Grandma Ella told it, she was at Rock Hill Baptist Church sitting beside her sister, Marie Goins Butler, when she noticed two half-white babies sitting on the choir. She whispered to her sister that people had a lot of nerve bringing their little half-white babies to church and sitting them on the choir. Marie said, "Sister Ella, I believe those are your grandbabies." Grandma said she kept on fussing until Marie told her, "Sister Ella, pull up your glasses," which were perched low on her nose. Grandma did and with joy declared to her sister, "Those are my little 'red' grandbabies." She began joyfully saying how cute they were, just a-singing, "You should have seen them."

When I was in Grandpa Saul and Grandma Ella's home, it was like a dream, living in luxury with plenty of food. There was no fighting between Grandpa and Grandma. Whatever Grandpa Saul wanted, he got. Grandma just hummed and laughed.

During one such retreat, I told Grandma Ella about "The Thing" that had been visiting me at night and would press down on my chest trying to smother me. My screams in the night had become widely known in the community. After listening to my story, Grandma Ella told me of a Mr. G. who was a nice man but turned evil when she refused to give him eggs to sell for his benefit. Grandma and Grandpa always closed doors tightly at night. Grandma Ella said Mr. G entered the house after he became invisible, and no one could hear or see him. According to her, Mr. G. marched himself into their bedroom, jumped on top of her, and tried to smother her. She fought him. Grandpa was asleep and did not wake up. Grandma said that when people turn themselves into an evil spirits, only the person they are after will feel their presence. Grandma Ella saw Mr. G. the next day. He could barely walk. Grandma told him if he came back again bothering her about some eggs, she would fix him where he would not be walking at all. After that threat, Grandma Ella said, he never returned to bother her.

I began to feel better after hearing Grandma's story. I was not imagining things. An evil spirit was real and one was after me. Mama was the only person who believed me. She would ask me questions often about The Thing. I told her it was a man, and he was dressed in black clothes. The belief in hants, ghosts, and evil spirits abounds in Longtown. I told Mama about my talk with Grandma Ella. Mama asked Daddy to sleep in my bed, and I slept with her. During the night, I heard sounds of movement on the back steps of our house. I woke Mama to tell her The Thing was coming. Then I heard the creaking of the door as it opened. I began to scream that The Thing was in the house. By now Daddy was awake, and Mama was screaming to Daddy to "catch it." Daddy said he grabbed at it but missed. He said The Thing looked like a cat. Mama opened the back door and yelled, "You better not come back here scaring my child. I will kill your ass." The Thing never returned.

After I had spent a few days with my grandparents, Mama and Daddy would come pick me up. It was well timed. Mama knew that after a few days I would no longer be a guest, and Grandpa Saul would expect me to fall in step with the work schedule on the farm. Grandpa Saul was known to be swift and vigorous with the strap. Mama was aware of this and vowed he was to never lay a hand on a child of hers. So she made sure that upon the expiration of my guest status, she and Daddy were there to get me. I was glad, too, because the handwriting was on the wall that Grandpa would grant no extensions of my status as "company."

The visits to Grandpa and Grandma's were precious. It provided a time for me to be alone in my sadness and dream of better days. Grandpa always encouraged me to do well in school. He lifted my spirits by telling me I was smart and not to grieve over the unkind words of others. Grandma Ella was so sweet. She was always ready to give you extra food or treat you to something. I felt so special and loved being in their presence.

One day, Mama sat me down and told me she was going to leave Daddy. She said she was tired of Daddy's abusive treatment of her and of his meanness toward Saul and David because of their dark skin. She had found someone to care for Freddie, Saul, and David. She would take MacArthur with her. Mama asked me if I wanted to go with her or stay with Daddy. I told Mama I loved them both and could not choose between them. I went on a crying spree, and nothing and no one could console me. One night I overheard Mama telling Daddy that she would not leave him now because I was going to cry myself to death. She said she knew me and I was not going to stop crying, and that she would not have her child dying because of their separation. Mama told Daddy, "I will leave you as soon as Lottie Mae leaves home. Mark my words."

Chapter 14 — Alberta, 1945

It was mid-February 1945, and Mama and Daddy were busy preparing the fields for planting the crops. School was still in session. The land was plowed, fertilized, and sowed, and other nutrients were being added to the soil. Cotton stalks had been knocked down, piled up, and burned. Seeds, fertilizer, and plow tools, as well as clothing, had been acquired from merchants in Ridgeway with the understanding that all debts would be paid with the first bales of cotton.

Mama and Daddy always hoped there would be enough money after paying their debts to buy clothes and shoes for everyone. Many times there was not. Times were tough, but Mama and Daddy continued to work, always hoping for a better day. In the late afternoon, Daddy would be off fishing until sundown. If successful, he brought home enough fish for several meals.

Mama had organized clothing for an expected sixth child. She had patched and sewn clothing, and put her house in order. In anticipation of another child, Grandpa Joe had added a room to the little house, which was partitioned to make a small kitchen and a sitting room. Mama, always looking ahead, wanted a sitting room to be available when I began to court.

Mama and Daddy, like most of their neighbors, worked hard but had little to show for their labor. The war was still on, and families continued to struggle to make ends meet. They plowed and planted the fields with the hope the new crops would yield more than last year's. There was always hope that a better day was coming, but no one seemed to know when it would arrive. People just continued to pray and work.

Despite hard times, there were joyous times. The birth of each child brought joy, even though feeding another mouth and providing clothing could pose a hardship. Mama and Daddy were looking forward to their new arrival to join Freddie, Saul, David, MacArthur, and me. There was a lot of speculation as to when another girl would join the family. Boys were highly valued because they made good field hands. So Daddy was not unhappy about having many boys, and Mama was not complaining because she had only one head to comb and plait. The only person making noise was my eight-year-old self. I was just sick of the boys. Because of the lack of space, all the children slept together. Mama arranged the children sideways in one bed. The boys were always kicking and pulling the covers. Whoever pulled the hardest was in control of the covers—that was Freddie and Saul. I did not fare well, as I was no match for the boys. They were a rough bunch, whether sleeping or playing. Eventually, I got my own cot, but I still had to compete with the boys for a quilt, as well as straw for my mattress. I did not fare well in this competition either.

I wanted a change in the makeup of the family and began praying for a little sister. I was treated like a princess by all except my brothers. Mama dressed me in cute little dresses and styled my hair in Shirley Temple curls. I was my father's pride and joy. Mama was not a seamstress like her sisters, but she got her Aunt Sina to make clothes for me.

On March 8, 1945, a baby girl was born, expanding the family to eight. The midwife suggested the name Alberta for Daddy's oldest brother Albert. I took a look at my little sister cuddled in Mama's arms.

Alberta had a thick head of tightly curled black hair. I was thrilled to have a little sister, but I did not ask to hold her.

Word spread quickly across Longtown and upper Kershaw County that Estelle and "Little Joe" (as he was called by most people) had a new baby—and it was a girl! The announcement of Alberta's birth brought many visitors. Everyone wanted to see the new baby. Is she healthy? Who does she favor? The new baby was scrutinized for hair type, skin color, big or small bone, nose, and potential personality based upon the moon's sign at time of birth. A person born in March is said to be changeable like the wind. You never know which way they are going to blow. Alberta was expected to have the persona of March.

The visitors found Alberta to be a pretty baby. It was not enough for them to make their observation. They would end their inspection by comparing the looks of the two girls. Who is the prettiest? The folks would seesaw back and forth, and finally begin a debate. "This child is going to be prettier than Lottie Mae," said Miss Sina. "I believe you are right, sister," echoed Miss Frances. Mr. Moses spoke up: "Well, well, you both are dead wrong, dead wrong! Lottie Mae looks like her Aunt Della. Just like her for the world. Now, there ain't a prettier woman than Della. No! No!" This debate went on much longer and more often than I liked.

As the months went by, I became upset that attention was shifting from me to the new baby, and resented having to listen to the comparisons. The next time the church ladies began their debate about who was the prettiest, I spoke up: "She may be the prettiest, but she is never going to wear Shirley Temple curls. That gal has some nappy hair." The old ladies got quiet, and when they resumed their conversation, they did not talk about who was the prettiest.

Mama returned to the field, and David began his child care apprenticeship with Alberta. David was old enough to begin doing a little work in the fields, but because of his asthma, he was assigned the role of babysitter.

No homes at Grandpa Joe's place or nearby neighbors had running water. Mama hung a bucket for slop on a nail outside the kitchen window to catch used water and other waste. One summer evening, Mama was busy preparing supper, a pot of boiled salt-cured ham. After the water came to a rolling boil, she opened the lid slightly, took the pot to the window and poured off the scalding water. Five-year-old Alberta was playing in the sand underneath the slop bucket with her newly found "friends," some large black ants, and Mama did not see her. Some of the scalding water spilled out of the slop bucket, landing on Alberta's shoulder and neck. She let out a chilling scream and began to run in many directions. Mama had difficulty catching and restraining her. It was a serious burn. Mr. Walter gave Mama a ride to Dr. Dobson, whose office was twelve miles away in Ridgeway.

Mama stayed up all night attending to Alberta's burn. Adding to Mama's pain, she could not make Alberta understand it was an accident. "You burned me," Alberta kept repeating, the words, piercing Mama's heart like a knife each time. "Baby, I didn't see you. I didn't mean to," Mama told her over and over. Alberta says she remembers the incident and how Mama kept her sitting upright all night so her neck would not draw up. Mama burned a white sheet, and put green ointment on the burn on her neck and arm. Alberta says that every time she sees a new doctor, they comment on how well Mama took care of her burns.

About a year later, Alberta ran into a barbed-wire fence and received a cut over her eye. On the farm, one has to watch out for farm animals, snakes, rabid dogs on the run, and wild foxes. There are a lot of barbed-wire fences to keep some critters in and others out. It was a goal not to get seriously injured. Getting to a doctor was not easy. There were very few cars. Mr. Walter, who lived near the Bell farm, was always willing to help in an emergency if he was available. He was the postman and the father of several children with Miss Libby.

While Alberta was being treated for the eye cut, the doctor asked if any of the other children had problems. Mama mentioned that MacArthur had a hard time seeing the cows in the field, so he was taken to have his eyes examined. When he put on his first pair of eyeglasses, he announced with enthusiasm, "Its daylight! I can see." It was a happy occasion for MacArthur and Mama. The family rejoiced. Although Mama, during her childhood, had guided her sister Scillar through the pastures and barnyard because of her poor eyesight, she had not given it a thought that her son could have a vision problem.

CHAPTER 15 — LILLIE, 1946

On a warm, sunny April day, Miss Mary Washington, the midwife, walked several miles to our parents' house to attend the birth of the couple's seventh child. Miss Mary did not have any other expecting mothers for the next couple of months, and Mama was ready to "go into the house" within a few days. Miss Mary loved visiting Cuzin Julia, Miss Red, and the other ladies in the area. This was a perfect time to catch up on the talk.

It was a busy time for the farmers, who had finished planting their crops of cotton, corn, potatoes, sweet potatoes, cabbage, collards, okra, string beans, pole beans, and turnips. The hogs for fall slaughter had been chosen, and the date set for their slow march to the smokehouse. The boll weevils were looking for a home in the cotton fields, and the farmers were on a warpath to make sure their stay would be cut short. Daddy and others were busy mixing DDT and other concoctions together to mop on the cotton plants. They had a sure solution for killing the boll weevils. The poison was so deadly it could kill animals and humans if it were swallowed.

Miss Mary was the midwife for all the children except me and was a favorite among the families in Longtown. She especially enjoyed assisting Mama because she was a very good housekeeper and always planned far ahead. The family's clothes had been washed, ironed, and repaired a couple of months in advance as she waited for the baby to arrive. She kept the yard swept and everything very neat. Everything the midwife would need was always available.

On the afternoon of April 28, 1946, a little, dark chocolate bundle arrived quietly. She had a beautiful head of hair. She did not create a lot of emotions or call attention to herself. People were still focusing on Alberta, the pretty one. By this time, I had discovered that little sisters could be a distraction and were too young for playmates. The new baby was placed in David's care, so now he had two small ones to care for.

Miss Maggie Derry looked at the baby and said, "Stell, name that child Lillian Blondell." Mama liked the name. She was tired of so many children named Mattie Mae, Lottie Mae, Annie Mae, Pearlie Mae, Missy Mae, Dottie Bell, Rosie Bell, and Lula Bell. *Shit, enough is enough*, she thought. No one in the family was named Lillian, and she made sure her child would not be called Lillie Mae or Lillie Bell. Why Miss Maggie Derry chose this name was a mystery.

Always known as the family detective, snoop, peanut thief, and cake spoiler, I went on to the Internet years later and came to the conclusion that Lillie was most likely named for actresses Lillian Gish and Joan Blondell. Both were enjoying successful movie careers around the time of Lillie's birth. I believe Miss Maggie Derry took the first name of Lillian Gish and the last name of Joan Blondell to create the unusual name.

The name Lillie seemed to be the perfect fit. Lily of the valley has strong roots and a fragrance that is sweet, calming, and uplifting. Easter lilies bring joy in the spring after a brutal winter, hope that new life awaits after life ends on one plane. Daylilies delight in midsummer when the heat is oppressive, opening a beautiful new flower every day.

CHAPTER 16 — HARD TIMES ARRIVE

In 1947, Daddy was suffering with great pain in his arm and was unable to work. It eventually became necessary to seek help with the farm. Mr. Jake, an old homeless man, agreed to work with our family in exchange for food, a pallet for sleeping on the kitchen floor, and a little change to spend on Saturday evening at the country store.

In 1948, Daddy went to the doctors at Columbia Hospital. He learned that the pain was from an old injury he received as a young boy. Daddy told the doctors he remembered falling off a mule. At the time, his parents rubbed his arm with ointments, and when that stopped easing the pain, he began taking many pain remedies. Eventually, the pain became unbearable. Daddy could not sleep. He began screaming in agony day and night. He had to have surgery to remove the decay from the arm.

As if our family did not have enough trouble with Daddy being ill and unable to work, I became ill with rheumatic fever. I was transported by the public health nurse, Miss Dove, to the Crippled Children Clinic in Columbia, where I underwent outpatient treatment. The doctors prescribed daily vitamins and complete bed rest. I was allowed to go to school, but was restricted from running and playing. I also could not work in the field. My brothers would complain about having to work in the hot sun while I stayed in the house and went to school.

In early 1949, Daddy was still recovering, and Mr. Jake had left without notice. Mama tried to secure supplies and food to last until harvest time under the same terms as Daddy and other farmers did. Farmers were given credit to purchase needed items and pay upon getting their first bale of cotton. The merchants refused to extend this practice to Mama; however, telling her "your husband must sign for credit." Mama told them she did not need her husband to sign for her, as she was the one doing the work. Mama was in a no-win situation. Merchants would not accept Daddy's signature either because he was unable to work. Mama vowed she would not patronize the merchants in Ridgeway and kept her promise for thirty-seven-plus years when a woman was elected mayor of Ridgeway. Mama got some money from friends, but it was not enough. Hard times had entered our house.

Daddy's brothers George and Albert would give food from time to time. They each had a large family. Daddy's father gave us nothing. Mama and Daddy were in a tough place. Their parents did not come to their rescue, although they had the means to help. They operated on the motto "root, little piggy, or die."

Grandpa Saul gave us some "bran" of the same quality that was fed to the hogs. Mama sifted and resifted the bran to separate the small amount of flour from the wheat hulls, but it was impossible to remove all the sharp hulls. Bread made with this flour would scratch our throats when we swallowed. But we were hungry, and with nothing else to eat, we ate the bread and cried. Mama soon joined us in this most unforgettable experience of human misery. We were living in America the beautiful!

Uncle Prince, Mama's youngest brother, made an unexpected visit and learned of our situation. He was very angry that we were hungry when there was food available. The next morning he returned with croker sacks full of food. Mama didn't ask how he was able to get so much food; he had no money and no transportation. She never forgot his generosity.

To add more stress, Mama was pregnant with Josephine, and with Daddy unable to work, it was she and Freddie, who was close to twelve years old, who did the plowing of the crops. It took the two with hands holding the plow together to penetrate the earth. The sight of Mama and Freddie trying to hold the plow in the hard, red clay ground was unforgettable.

Mama tried to get public assistance but was denied. She was told there was a twelve-year-old boy in the family who was old enough to work the farm. Mama was hurt that anyone in their right mind could think a twelve-year-old could run a farm. We were given used clothes such as tennis outfits, swimsuits, and riding outfits with matching caps—nothing practical for farm life.

CHAPTER 17 — JOSEPHINE - 1949

At the time Mama was pregnant with Josephine, I was nearly thirteen, Freddie was just short of twelve, and Saul was eleven. There was still work to be done. All through her last months of pregnancy, Mama did the plowing and other chores. Josephine was born on August 8, 1949. Daddy asked that this daughter be named Josephine. He had lost early battles to name a son for him; Mama always objected, saying there were too many Josephs in the family. This time they were in agreement.

As the baby of the family, Josephine was special from the start. She became Mama's companion on long drives around the countryside. No one knew where they went, as Mama refused to tell and no one could bribe Josephine to tell.

Times had been hard for our family. Daddy still was unable to work, as he was still recovering from surgery. I was recovering from rheumatic fever. In addition to the farming, during the winter months, Freddie assisted Mama with washing clothes and cutting firewood, which involved scraping ice off the fallen trees before cutting them to fireplace length. Freddie was right when he proclaimed he had worked for as long as he could remember.

Saul was expected to willingly follow in Freddie's footsteps. He, too, had the chore of plowing the fields, but unlike Freddie, he complained vehemently, saying the ground was too hard. Saul did not apply the full manual strength needed to dig the plow deep into the red clay earth, and hold it there sufficiently long to break the earth apart and till acres of land. No amount of coaching could get him to do this laborious work in the manner needed.

When Mama threatened Saul with a whipping, you knew he was in for a memorable one. We children knew from experience that you did not want a whipping from Mama. The large, stinging switch would make an ordinary person shiver in pain just looking at it. Saul was not moved by the threat of a whipping, however. Mama, not to be outdone by her child, threatened him with death. Saul calmly told her he didn't care if she killed him, saying he would not have to plow. Now Mama was upset. She thought, "What kind of fool child have I given birth to?" It was time for a new strategy. Little did she know, Saul had his own plan.

He promised he would work hard if he got a new bike. So a deal was struck between a determined mother and her stubborn son. At harvest time, Saul received his new bike. He was filled with joy. He had accomplished his goal, a feat many boys desired but were too fearful to attempt: extort from a parent a bike for doing what others were told they must do without compensation.

Saul got his new bike, and off he went, peddling at high speed, kicking up red dust along the way, and nearly knocking down old man Dave. The old man yelled to Saul: "You are not going to have good luck with that bike." Saul yelled back, "I am sorry," and continued on his way. On Saul's return from the store, Mr. Dave stood in the middle of the road, and as Saul prepared to go past him, he yelled, "Stop!" And Saul did. Mr. Dave told Saul he had struck him and not apologized. Mr. Dave pointed his finger at the bike and repeatedly said to Saul, "You will never have good luck with the bike." Within days, the bike began to come apart, first one thing and then another. It could not be repaired. The children were convinced that Mr. Dave's spell caused the bike's deterioration.

Not long afterward, the neighbors gathered at Mr. Dave's house. Mr. Dave had been killed when he was thrown by his mule, Danger, so named for his stubborn and combative behavior. Mr. Dave and Danger had similar personality traits, and people whispered that it appeared Danger got the best of Mr. Dave in their tug of war. One neighbor even suggested that Mr. Dave would be back to settle his score with Danger.

The children gathered outside and discussed the adults' comments. Each child had a story to tell of an encounter with Mr. Dave. He was described as the meanest man who ever lived and ever died. He terrorized the children with threats of casting spells upon them. He told how he could turn them into rocks, turtles, foxes, or rabbits if he wanted to and that they would never see their parents or friends again. He dared them to cross him or step on the side of the road where his house stood. Every child dreaded when it was his or her turn to go to the store, for there was no other way except to pass Mr. Dave's house. They would tremble with fear and pray he would not be on his porch.

Now that Mr. Dave had died, Saul felt good and thought it was about time the evil old man had croaked. When he told Sammy and Buster how he felt, they warned him that Mr. Dave might return, just as the adults said he would. Saul shrugged his shoulders, said no one returned from the dead, and went home.

Late in the night, Saul heard a knocking, first lightly and then louder. It grew louder and louder, but no one else seemed to hear it. The dogs did not bark and Daddy kept snoring. Saul wondered what was making the noise. Then he recalled that Sammy and Buster said that dead people could return, and no one but the person they were making contact with could see or hear them. He began to shiver. Could Mr. Dave be paying him a visit? The knocking grew louder still, and he was sure he heard footsteps on the back steps, yet still there were no sounds from the dogs and his father's snoring continued uninterrupted. Saul's heart began to pound, the bed started shaking, and he began to sweat. *No! No! It can't be Mr. Dave!* Just then the bedroom door slammed shut, and he jumped up in his bed, screaming and begging Mr. Dave not to take him away. Mama and Daddy rushed to his side and calmed him down. Daddy closed the window as Mama got Saul a glass of milk. Everyone returned to bed.

By the time Josephine arrived, David had become an experienced and loving babysitter. Of the three brothers, David was the kindest to the three young sisters. He also became their protector from our brother Saul, also known as "Solomon Grundy." Saul made war against them while MacArthur focused on his own survival. Saul punched, pinched, and did everything he could think of that would make the three sisters' lives painful and miserable. They would run to David for cover. Saul would brazenly reach behind David to execute punishment on them. After a while, David got tired and challenged him. Life became easier for the girls and MacArthur. But whenever they were found away from their home base, "Solomon Grundy" would strike.

David became a father figure to Alberta, Lillie, and Josephine. Josephine even called him *Daddy*. Because of Mama's work schedule, David would braid his sisters' hair and help get them ready for school. He took Josephine to school with him. By this time, I was in high school, and Saul and Freddie had quit school to work the farm.

When Freddie, Saul, MacArthur, and I later went north, David remained at home. There was plenty of work for him, as he was the only male left. He helped work a large vegetable garden, and assisted in the caring for the cows, goats, chickens, and mules. He instructed the girls in many farm activities, including corn shucking; pulling and bundling fodder; building storage banks to hold sweet potatoes over the winter; pulling peanuts and spreading them on the tin roof of the house for curing; and cutting, bundling, and transporting sugar cane for processing at Grandpa Solomon Stone's farm. David also was responsible for seeing that there was plenty of water for cooking and washing clothes. The spring was quite a distance from the house, a half mile. When there were long periods between rainfalls, he hitched the mule to a sled and drove to the spring to fetch large barrels of water. Alberta, Lillie, and Josephine would accompany him, not so much to help fill the barrels, but because they loved to ride on the sled. David took great care to make sure they held on to the barrels tightly and that the mule pulled the sled gently and slowly.

Playing was a wonderful pastime, when time could be found. As the years went by, the girls grew and attended grade school, then high school. Farm life began to change for all.

Chapter 18 — Thanksgiving At Grandparents' House

Despite the hard times, there were good times. Thanksgiving was a special time of the year. Mama's parents had dinner at their home for all their children, grandchildren, other relatives, and friends. It was a picture of the Pilgrims' first Thanksgiving, as seen in our textbooks, except the Indians did not come. The men would hunt for game, and the women cooked and baked. Grandpa Saul always slaughtered a calf or pig. Aunt Janie and Aunt Lela would make fancy pies and cakes.

The menu included turkey, stuffing, roast pork and beef, cooked rutabagas, mashed white turnip, and corn bread. The food was plentiful and delicious.

The children played games such as hopscotch and Here We Go Round the Mulberry Bush. We sang "Little Liza Jane" and "Little Sally Walker"; there was a lot of shaking it to the east, shaking it to the west, and shaking it to the one you loved the best. The teenage girls talked about boys and who had begun their menstrual cycle. If you had not begun, you were too young to be in their company. The boys would go bareback riding on the mules. They would take the animals to the watering hole, then race back to the barn.

When the table had been set for dinner, Grandpa Saul would have everyone line up. He wanted to see how far a single line would go, and it extended past Uncle McKinley and Aunt Baby Ruth's house. The longer the line, the happier he would be. The line became so long that not everyone could hear the grace when it was said, so Grandpa Saul required everyone to recite a Bible verse before picking up his or her plate to get food. Grandpa Saul did not tell anyone how long the Bible verse had to be. We heard an abundance of "Jesus wept." He praised each person after his or her recitation. I always wanted to be a shining star for Grandpa Saul, so I departed from the chorus of "Jesus wept" and said, "Wait on the Lord and be of good courage. Wait, I say, on the Lord." Grandpa Saul was indeed pleased and asked everyone nearby to stop and listen as he asked me to repeat the verse, and I did so willingly. Grandpa sang praises, telling everyone that it was quite a nice Bible verse.

CHAPTER 19 — MAMA REBELS

By 1950, it was clear that farming was not going to put food on the table, so Daddy found work at Dupont near Camden, South Carolina. He drove about twenty-four miles a day, five days a week. The farm work was left to Mama and the children, but every Saturday during the harvesting season, Daddy loaded the cotton on the wagon, took it to the gin house, sold it, and kept the money. He started spending his money on booze and lying to Mama about how much he was paying for food. He took advantage of Mama because she could not add and subtract the way he could. I was now in high school and didn't have enough money to buy lunch in the cafeteria. I told Mama how Daddy was spending the money. Mama was not happy and confronted Daddy about his behavior. She felt she and the children worked to produce the crops and Daddy just took the money and spent it. We had hoped our circumstances would change.

Daddy became more and more aggressive as time went by. Mama made up her mind to fight back, verbally and physically. She was not going to run, and she was not going to take any more "shit" from Daddy. She had taken as much as she was going to take from him and his "foolishness."

Soon, root doctors entered. Daddy accused Mama of having root doctors put spells on him, so he began spending his money on root doctors to give him something to counteract whatever it was that Mama supposedly was doing to him. Mama did not have money, but she was sweet and likable. The same root doctors who were selling the roots to Daddy gave them to Mama for free. Her women friends also would help her out. Our house was in turmoil!

Guns then came into our home, with both parents bearing arms and swearing they would not back down. The older children became detectives and watched Mama and Daddy like a chicken hawk watched the chickens. We wanted to make sure we knew where the guns were at all times. One of us once disabled a pistol so it would not fire. We worked to keep one parent from killing the other. There was a lot of crying and a lot of fear. We loved our parents and wanted no harm to come to either.

MIGRATION

CHAPTER 20 — MAMA MAKES HER MOVE

Mama had decided enough was enough. She decided on a game plan to get Daddy out of the house and up the road to Washington, D.C., with his brother. Mama wrote the script, and she rehearsed it with us. We children became good stage players as all our lives depended upon it. What we said and how we said it was important. We played our roles magnificently. Daddy fell into the trap that Mama had set.

First, Mama covered the peepholes in the barn from the inside, locked the door, and refused to give Daddy the key. When Daddy asked us how much cotton we had picked in an effort to learn whether we were nearing a bale, we replied we didn't know. Mama had taught us there was no shame in saying "I don't know.""

Mama's next move was to get the cotton to the gin house without Daddy knowing we had picked a bale. As soon as Daddy left for work, the wagon was loaded and she set off to the gin house with the boys. She sold the cotton and would not give Daddy any of the money. Mama told Grandpa Joe that his agreement regarding use of the farmland was between him and his son. She would not give up any money except to pay what was owed to the merchants.

Chapter 21 — Daddy Moves North

In 1955, a cousin visiting from Connecticut suggested that Daddy move there where work was plentiful. Living in Connecticut, Daddy would not as easily be able to pick up and come home for a weekend. So that summer Mama began orchestrating Daddy moving on. She instructed us how to behave. We were not to seem glad he was leaving, but no sadness either because then he might decide not to go. We could not have that. Daddy had to move on. We went into neutral drive while Mama worked her magic. Before the end of the year, Daddy left for Connecticut. Mama got a full-time job at South Carolina State Hospital, near Columbia.

I married Clyburn Scott, son of Dave Scott and Elease Bennett Scott, in the spring of 1956. Upon learning of my pregnancy, I said I wanted to have the baby in the hospital. My husband objected, saying the cost of delivering at a hospital was too much when a midwife could assist the delivery for far less. He said other women did not have a problem using midwives, and he was not going to be the laughing stock of Fairfield and Kershaw Counties. If a midwife was good enough for others, he said, they were good enough for me.

I was still traumatized from the death of my friend Mary, who had married Uncle Prince and died in childbirth at age fifteen. Some said the midwife waited too long to seek assistance. I did not care what the reason was—I wanted to have my baby in the hospital. So I went on a crying jag. Mama told Daddy that I was crying and was going to cry myself to death. Mama said she was not going to stand for this. Daddy agreed to send money home regularly and pay all costs. It was not long afterward other women began to go to the hospital to have their babies too. "If Lottie Mae can go to the hospital to have her baby, I can too," they said, and they did. A trailblazer had emerged from the red clay fields of Longtown.

I had many false labor pains. Mama made many fifty-mile trips to take me to Dr. McCants. After getting out of his bed so frequently to attend to me because of false labor pains, he yelled, "This gal is going to stay here until she has the baby." He called his nurse and told her she was to keep me until delivery time. "I got work to do," he said. Mama was upset and thought he was being unfair to his nurse, who had work of her own to do also. The nurse's response to Mama: "Dr. McCants has ordered me to take care of Lottie Mae, and that is what I am going to do." That was exactly what she did.

Clyburn Scott Jr. was born October 23, 1956, and given the nickname Bill by his maternal grandfather, Joe Bell, who had paid for the prenatal care as well as hospitalization for his grandchild's delivery.

While I was in the hospital, Mama moved the family off Grandpa Joe's land. She said her grandchild would not begin his life in a house without electricity and proudly brought him to a new home with electricity at Stewart's Place which was closer to Ridgeway. Daddy discovered on his next visit to South Carolina that he had no home there that could be called his own. Mama was in her house, and she made it clear to Daddy that it was her house. He could visit but could not spend the night, and he had no say about how she ran her house. The marriage had ended. Daddy, in a demanding voice, said he wanted a divorce.

Mama, in an equal tone of voice, told him no, and should he die first, she would draw his social security.

When all was done and said, Mama and Daddy were a team when it came to their children. They joined forces to make sure that their first grandchild was born in a hospital. Daddy sent money on a regular basis for Mama to save for the doctor and hospital bills. Later, they agreed it was best for me to leave my husband and move to Connecticut with my six-month-old son. Through all the turmoil with Daddy, Mama reminded us that he was our father. She said what happened between them had nothing to do with us. She reminded us that the Bible says, "Honor your father and mother."

Chapter 22 — Freddie Moves North

In 1954, the family ceased farming. It no longer provided sufficiently for the family's needs. Freddie went to work picking corn for twenty dollars a week. He gave all the money to Mama, who gave him two dollars a week to spend for himself. He never complained, as the money was needed to help the family. When Mama said she didn't have another child like Freddie, she was right.

In 1956 Freddie moved to Connecticut with Daddy. He immediately found work at Yantic Grain where Daddy was working. With a job paying him money, a whole new life emerged for Freddie. Freddie formed a relationship with Betty Holland. They had three children, Paulette, Freddie, and Yvette. Later he married Dorothy Valdlez and became the father of Alfredo, Kevin, and Janine. Like a rolling stone, he then moved to Boston, Massachusetts, where he met and married Dorothy Mae Rhone. Her two sons, Tony and Greg, became his sons and they had three children: Cynthia, Gerald, and Jacquelyn. He and Dorothy Mae settled in Pawcatuck, Connecticut. Freddie became a master car body workman known for his superior work.

Dorothy Mae and Freddie began to host yearly birthday events for themselves. Whenever the opportunity presented itself, Freddie was ready for a party. He told how he met Diana Ross in Boston, and took her and others singers to dinner and showed them a good time. Some laughed and said it did not happen. I said it did, and the reason was because Freddie was good looking. He was an impeccable dresser, had a pocket full of money, and was willing to spend it. Freddie wore an infectious smile that said, "Follow me, and I will show you a good time." When he took the dance floor with his partner, others would stop and watch the show.

Chapter 23 — Saul, Lottie Mae, and Baby Clyburn

It was April 8, 1957, a warm, sunny day in Ridgeway, South Carolina. The spring flowers were in full bloom. Farmers had planted their crops of corn, cotton, sweet potatoes, and other vegetables. It was a busy time for everyone, including the small children who were busy keeping weeds out of the garden and fields. Saul was eighteen. I had separated from my husband, Clyburn Scott, in early March. Saul and I were busy packing our few belongings in brown paper bags for a long journey north.

We had heard many stories about life in Connecticut from our brother Freddie. One could easily find a job in the shoe factory or doing housework. The pay was good. One did not have to say "Yes, Ma'am" or "Yes, Sir" to white people, and especially to their children. We had repeatedly heard of the freedoms in New York, New Jersey, and Connecticut: freedom to do what you desired, eat where you choose, and try on shoes before purchasing them. Life up north seemed to be a dream we could not wait to experience.

On the day of departure, Saul and I did no work. We went to the nearby farms to give goodbyes to friends and relatives. Everyone wished us well but told us not to return with a Northern accent and acting all "proper." At about 8 P.M., Daddy, Freddie, and I, with six-month-old baby Bill in my arms, got into the 1957 Buick belonging to Mr. Buddy Murphy. Mr. Buddy always drove a new car to South Carolina. He was a very peculiar person. He made few stops between South Carolina and Connecticut; he stopped only for gas. Saul rode with Timothy Howard, and on this particular trip it took twenty-five hours because of the frequent stops Mr. Howard was making. He was having trouble with the driving on this occasion.

Saul and I brought along fried chicken, sweet potato pie, biscuits, and Kool-Aid. Mama had prepared a hefty meal for our long trip. Before the journey to Connecticut, the farthest Saul and I had traveled was twenty-three miles to Columbia.

We arrived in Connecticut on April 9, 1957. After riding all night, Saul went to Yantic Grain at 7 A.M. looking for work. He was hired immediately, joining Daddy and Freddie. Daddy, Saul, Freddie, baby Clyburn Jr., and I lived in a one-bedroom apartment on the third floor.

I did some housework and worked briefly at Werman Shoe Factory, where many people from Longtown had found work. Between the cost of childcare and lack of reliability of sitters, I had a hard time making ends meet. Mama offered to help by caring for my son until I got on my feet. I accepted Mama's help. Clyburn and I later divorced.

I deliberately had only one child. I had observed many women getting stuck in unhappy marriages, unable to leave because of the children. You can't just pick up and leave. Grandparents and other relatives sometimes would step up to care for children whose mothers had to leave to save their own lives, but usually if you left without your children, someone else would raise them and they would never become yours. I never regretted having only one child; however, I do regret the separation from my son during the early years.

CHAPTER 24 — ALBERTA, LILLIE, AND JOSEPHINE

After graduation from high school in 1962, Alberta moved to Connecticut to live with Daddy. She had wanted to live with me, but Mama forbade it, saying, "I am not going to send my child to live with you for you to kill her." Mama knew her daughters and that there would be a personality clash between the two of us. Alberta found work at a nursing home. Later, she attended a secretarial program at the Norwich Commercial College, where I also attended.

It soon became very clear what Mama feared. Alberta was testy and not inclined to listen to her "big" sister. We got into an argument. Alberta told me she would "fix" me by running up the phone bill in my name by making long-distance calls throughout the country all night long. Not to be outdone, I called the phone company and requested the service be disconnected immediately. Within ten minutes, Alberta had a dead phone. She called from the neighbor's phone screaming and accusing me of being mean.

Alberta and her friends Gail and Ann were the "dancing queens." Every day after work, they would gather at Daddy's apartment and dance all evening. The linoleum was worn bare from their dancing.

Daddy would point out the spot where they danced, complaining that they had worn out his linoleum. He did this for all visitors. They had to see the spot where the girls danced. While Daddy complained to everyone who would listen, he loved every minute of the girls dancing. It also gave him an excuse not to buy new linoleum. "Little Joe" was as tight with his money as his father, "Old Man Joe Bell."

The three girlfriends enjoyed each other's company. They loved going to the nightclubs, although they were underage. The bartenders would allow them to party for a little while, and when the place began to get crowded, they would be shown the door. New London was across the river from the submarine base. It was a great place for meeting the sailors. Alberta became a mother. Her daughter Michelle arrived, and Alberta returned to work, unlike most unwed mothers who went on welfare. She had an excellent sitter for Michelle named Viola.

Before long, Alberta announced to me that Charles Dortch had proposed marriage. I, like Mama, thought Alberta was moving too fast, especially with a divorced man who had to pay child support for two children. Charles arrived at my house and promised that he would take good care of Alberta and Michelle. With that, "big sister folded her hands." I wished the couple happiness and helped Alberta prepare for the wedding. It was a lovely wedding, attended by a small group of family and a few friends in the home of Mrs. Isabelle Dortch, Charles's mother. Her home had antique furniture passed down from her grandparents. Alberta and Charles soon had two children: Thomas first, then Angela. Charles was shocked that his daughter had the same name as that woman Angela Davis I liked so well, but it was too late to change as her birth certificate had already been signed and submitted.

In 1962, Joyce Kirkland arrived from Longtown. Saul and Joyce were married, and they had three children: Jervis, Terri, and Solomon. In 1964, Lillie married John L. Jackson, and they moved to Washington, D.C., where they raised their three children: Thomas, Derwin, and Marilyn.

MacArthur spent short visits in Connecticut, but he returned home after becoming lonely for his love, Jessie Mae Butler, who was not leaving South Carolina for love or money. MacArthur and Jessie Mae raised four children: Reecy, Dwayne, Wade, and Darryl.

David had shown no signs of moving to Connecticut. He was too busy having fun. Then he met Lillie Davis Harrison, a widow with three children, and his "wild" life ended. They had one child, Pamela. David also became the father of Carolyn Belton from a previous relationship.

Now it was just Josephine at home living with Mama. This was an awakening for both Mama and Josephine. While Mama held a full-time job at the state hospital, she relied on Alberta, Lillie, and Josephine to do the daily chores at home. Mama had become accustomed to having dinner ready upon her arrival home from work. Lillie did most of the cooking. Alberta did some cooking and cleaning, but always took a "beauty" nap. When not studying, Josephine spent her time beautifying the yard. The girls had made sure all of the work lived up to Mama's standard of perfection, which was very much in keeping with her daddy's ways. Now that Alberta and Lillie were gone, Mama still expected to find a cooked meal when she arrived home after work. Josephine was excellent at cleaning the house, but Mama discovered Josephine didn't know how to cook. One day when Mama returned home from working in a hot kitchen all day, she found a burnt meal. She was furious. Mama, like her daddy, would fuss up a storm when things were not done the right way. It was a long, silent journey, but as time passed, Josephine learned to cook. She wowed us all, including Mama, with her cooking.

Chapter 25 — From The Cotton Fields To The Boardroom

I soon found work as a salad counter girl at the Wauregan Hotel. There I met Charles Wright, who was the chef. He took time to show me how to prepare a salad plate. I did not last long at the job, though, because I had entered a workplace environment of which I had no understanding.

Wanda, the head waitress, did not like me from the beginning. She spoke to me in a snapping manner. She would snatch things out of my hand and speak rudely to me when requesting a modification of a salad plate. The other waitresses began to whisper among themselves. One day Wanda snatched a dirty plate out of my hand and took it to the owner, saying I had been served food on dirty plates and that I had become a distraction to Charles. I was fired immediately. Charles was shocked. Shortly thereafter, Wanda was gone. It was not long before Charles and I became husband and wife.

Meanwhile, I became restless. I began to pursue my dream of becoming a secretary and enrolled in Norwich Commercial College to take secretarial courses to increase my job opportunities. Visits to see my son in South Carolina once in a while were not enough; I wanted him back. Bill had settled in, however. He was Mama's baby and

Josephine's little brother. His uncles carried him everywhere in their arms. Everyone was happy with the arrangement except me. In addition to the stress of school, I began not feeling well. Mama was concerned I would have more stress trying to care for my son, so she brought along Cousin Norvice to help care for Bill while I went to school. It was crying time, with Mama leading the way.

I was elated to have Bill back in Norwich with me, but his response was, "Who are you?" When Mama returned to South Carolina, he cried daily, saying he wanted his "mama." There was more crying, as I could not make him understand I was his mother. While I regret being apart from him, on the other hand, I did not have the resources at the time to care for him alone.

Adding further confusion, Charles announced he did not like the nickname *Bill* and henceforth my son would be called *Billy*. It stuck like glue. However, some people began to call him William. When they were told his name was Clyburn, they expressed surprise, as Clyburn had no connection to the nickname Billy, which was a nickname for William. They wanted to know why the beautiful blue, green, and gray eyes on this brown-skinned child. They would stop, stare, and ask questions. In Longtown, the color of his eyes would not have drawn any attention. We were accustomed to seeing brown-skinned babies with blue and gray eyes.

After completing sufficient courses at Norwich Commercial College to become eligible for secretarial work, I went job seeking, but no one seemed interested in hiring me, despite my skills. Although I received a good score on a City of Norwich test I took, the city did not offer me a position. A staff member at the college had forewarned that I would not get the job. A partner of a prominent law firm was not interested in my skills but hired my classmates. The attorney told me that he had black friends and named them. I later learned that they were his clients.

The biggest blow in my search for work was when I applied at a local bank. After hearing I was seeking work, the bank president rushed out of his office and came face-to-face with me, saying, "There is no work here for you. There will never be work here for you." Then he waved his arms in a "scatting" and "shooing" motion in front of me to get out. It was the most humiliating experience. I was so stunned that I backed out of the door, then turned and ran crying all the way home to 50 Union Street. I sat down at my typewriter with tears falling and began to type, "I can and I will. I can and I will." I remembered the story of Will and Can't as told by our teacher, Miss Maggie Derry, at Mount Olive School. Can't said he could not climb the hill, and he did not. Will said he could climb the hill, and he did. Miss Maggie Derry urged her students to never say "can't." I knew I would succeed in finding work in an office.

After passing a clerk typist examination for the State of Connecticut, I was hired in 1962 at the Norwich State Hospital. My supervisor was age sixty-nine, and prior to my coming on board, he had hired four white women for his unit: three in their sixties and one in her fifties, all either widows or never married, and all with excellent work experience. I had no clerical work experience. The unit was known as the "Office of Rejects." Upon reaching the mandatory retirement age, the supervisor left. It was rumored that his request for an extension was denied because of his hiring decisions.

During my search for work, I became very aware of the difference between the North and South. In South Carolina, you learned early about the separation between the races. You would not bother to inquire about housing in certain areas; there was no pretending. Up north, you were led to believe there were no barriers to job opportunities, housing, and school. But while you could sit at food counters, it did not go unnoticed when a white person moved away when you sat next to them. One restaurant on the Westside of Norwich, Lincoln Inn, did not welcome blacks. After serving black people, they would break the glasses they drank from right in front of them. Norwich at this time also had issues with its police department. Black people believed they were being treated unfairly and this resulted in mistrust.

As I searched for housing, I quickly learned that white landlords would smile sweetly while telling you the recently advertised apartment had just been rented, apologetic about missing the opportunity to rent it to you. When a white person inquired just minutes later, they would be told the apartment was still available. It was not long before I became active in a fair housing group to help break down barriers of discrimination in Norwich.

In October 1963, my son Clyburn and I became charter members of the Norwich NAACP. Under the tutelage of Linwood Bland and Clarence Faulk, I began as chair of the Labor and Industry Committee to open doors of employment for blacks. I served as secretary of the branch and six years as president. Linwood was a fierce advocate for dismantling racism. He sought to tear down barriers wherever he found them. I learned from him that you could not close your eyes. You had to be vigilant twenty-four hours a day, seven days a week. You worked until midnight and went to work early the next morning at your day job. After working all day, you began "justice for all" work upon arriving home. We worked on getting the board of the Thames Valley Council for Community Action to amend its bylaws to require a representative from each of the New London and Norwich NAACP branches to serve on the board. My quest for equality in all aspects of American life has spanned more than sixty years.

Norvice Bell spent her first Christmas in Norwich with my family and me and said it was the best Christmas she'd ever had. I agreed it was good; I was working and was able to buy gifts. Charles was a generous person, and Billy received lots of toys. Norvice later moved to Washington, D.C., to be near her sisters Mary and Martha, who had come north to live with relatives in pursuit of opportunities unavailable to them in South Carolina.

Though Charles was a wonderful person and provided well for the family, over time we had conflicts. He wanted to eat dinner at home and then watch TV. I wanted to go out to dinner. I wanted to go to New York City to eat and see shows. He did not, saying he had seen all the places and things he wanted to see. I fired back that I had not. The twenty-year difference in our ages was not an issue for me. I loved him, and he loved me. It was his refusal to engage in what I considered a full life that caused problems. The marriage ended, but our friendship continued.

Working at the Norwich State Hospital was a good experience. I learned various job tasks and had the opportunity to work in the office of the business manager when his secretary was absent. The crown jewel came when I was selected to work in the office of the superintendent, Dr. Morgan Martin, during his secretary's vacation. It was a big deal to be chosen to work in the front office. I also was part of the hospital team for the United Way campaign. There were mumbles when Dr. Martin asked me to join him for a photo connected to the campaign, and the photo appeared in the *Norwich Bulletin*.

While working at Norwich Hospital, I gained good insight into how cleverly white people worked to deny a black person a job opportunity. I applied for a clerk position at a level higher than the one I was in. I passed the test and was placed on the promotional list, which was a list of current employees eligible to fill a position. Another list contained the names of eligible nonemployees. The hiring person had the choice of requesting either a promotional list or a nonemployee list. I learned that, before requesting a list, my white male supervisor asked current white employees eligible for the promotion if they were interested in it. When they all said no, he chose the outside list, thereby by-passing me for the opportunity. This was being "slick." I had no grounds to complain because I was not on the list from which he chose to fill the vacancy.

I became friends with some wonderful employees at Norwich Hospital. When I wanted to purchase a car, Julie, a co-worker, told me what bank to go to and with whom to speak. This was at a time when women had trouble getting credit. She told me to speak only to the treasurer of the bank and to give my bank book to him at the start of our conversation. I followed her advice. The treasurer was impressed with my savings habit and granted the loan.

Around 1970, I left Norwich Hospital and went to work as a neighborhood resource worker for the Connecticut Commission on Human Rights and Opportunities. This was a golden opportunity. I worked twenty-two years for the commission, advancing to regional manager.

In 1980, I was named a corporator of The William W. Backus Hospital and, two years later, a trustee. In November 1988, I was elected chair of the Board of Trustees. In the midst of all of this, I completed college at the University of Connecticut and received a bachelor's degree. I traveled a longer road to become chair of Backus Hospital's Board of Trustees than my predecessors in that office. Among other differences, I was not a native New Englander and I wasn't chosen from among the leaders of the local business or legal establishments.

Chapter 26 — Climbing Jacob's Ladder

Freddie left school at age fourteen and never returned. He never learned to read, so he claimed. However, like Grandpa Joe, no one is known to cheat him out of a penny. He urged his children, and all children he came in contact with, to learn. His children heeded his advice and passed the message along to their children. Freddie is hailed as a master of mechanical bodywork.

Saul quit school before completing grade school, as he was needed to do farm work. After arriving in Connecticut, he went to Yantic Grain as a laborer. Then he was trained as a welder at Electric Boat, a division of General Dynamics, where he worked until he retired. In 1987, Saul received his GED certificate. He said you are never too old to learn and that education is important. He passed this message along to his children and others.

Saul purchased a computer for his granddaughter Tina while she was still in elementary school. This computer could meet not only the needs of a high school or college student, but those of a small business. He spared no expense because he envisioned that people who were not computer literate, and beyond, would miss out on opportunities and be unable to compete in tomorrow's workplace. Saul did not express the old saying, "I worked for what I got, and you gotta work for yours."

Rather, his gift was one of love and of pride. He wanted Tina to be able to compete with other students. He knew this could happen only if she were provided with the proper tools and support to aid her quest for self-sufficiency.

Saul and Joyce urged their children Terri, Solomon, and Jervis to continue their education beyond high school. All three children and their children are successful in their chosen fields. Saul's idol was his grandfather Solomon Stone, whom he fondly called a wise man like King Solomon. With the assistance of David Belton, Grandpa Saul learned how to access government services to build a modern farm. He owned his own farm when most black folks were sharecroppers. He was called Mr. Saul Stone when most black folks were called by their first names.

David went back to school to get his GED certificate. He continued to learn, and to support and inspire his children in pursuing their education. They are successful and are imparting to their offspring the same message: Education is essential.

MacArthur attended adult education classes and received a GED certificate. He and Jessie Mae insisted upon their children continuing their education. They did not have money for traditional colleges but decided that learning a skill at a technical college would be beneficial. All four children are graduates of Midlands Technical College and enjoying successful careers.

When Angela became pregnant with Alberta's first grandchild and wanted to quit college, Alberta "put her foot down" and told Angela she was going back to school. Angela thanks her mother for the "kick" as she now enjoys a successful career. She and her brother continue to inspire their children to move on up a little higher.

Lillie and her husband gifted the world with three wonderful children. Growing up, we were taught to distrust and fear the police. This opinion changes when your loved one puts on a police uniform. We cry and pray when they must wear riot gear and carry a body shield for their own protection as they work to protect all citizens.

Josephine has been our shining star. We knew she was smart and special from the beginning. She talked little, but observed her surroundings and the goings-on of others. She was the first to graduate from college, receiving her Bachelor of Arts from Voorhees College in 1971. We were so thrilled. She wanted to continue college to get a master's degree, which she did; she graduated from Syracuse University with a Master of Public Administration in 1972. Some of us said she wanted to make a career of going to school instead of getting a job. Her first child, James, arrived, but she continued her education. She married Sam Selph, and her second child, Brian, was born. Josephine then went off to the University of South Carolina, School of Law, graduated in 1988, and became a practicing attorney.

Josephine's son, James, graduated from the University of South Carolina, and following in his mother's footsteps, he attended law school, and is a practicing attorney in New York City. At his graduation from law school, Mama rocked in her seat during the entire ceremony, whispering repeatedly, "They said he couldn't do it, but he did." It was a joyful occasion.

STAYING CONNECTED

CHAPTER 27 — VACATIONING IN SOUTH CAROLINA

Family members made yearly trips to South Carolina to visit family members. In the springtime, Saul and Freddie would travel to fish, each time returning with large coolers filled with white perch and other types of fish. In August, Saul and Joyce made their yearly journey to attend the traditional picnic held the second Saturday of the month in the White Oak area. This tradition dates back as long as we can remember. Going to the picnic guaranteed they would see family members who still lived in the area, as well as visit friends and relatives from the North who took the trip for fellowship and to talk about the past and the present. There was lots of good food and the traditional annual baseball game. Fall was deer hunting time, and Saul and Freddie went to South Carolina to hunt. They never returned empty-handed and would bring back many stories of who shot what, when, and how. There was plenty of meat to share with family and friends.

During their Christmas gathering in Connecticut with friends and family, the table was full with turkey, ham, sliced deer meat, deer stew, and raccoon roasted to perfection. While South Carolina transplants were delighted to devour this delicious fare, our white guests screamed and laughed. They could not believe we were eating raccoon.

At down-home gatherings of Southern friends and family, I always had a story to tell about whites up north not appreciating good meat. I was invited to the home of a white schoolteacher to discuss fair housing. During the meeting, the lady suddenly invited everyone to look out on the porch. It was filled with raccoons of various sizes eating their dinner. She was so proud of her raccoons. I stood there knowing what a delicious meal they would make, but there was no way to separate the raccoons from the schoolteacher. Mama's words rushed into my head: "White people have a fool way of looking at things." Looking longingly at the raccoons, I agreed.

CHAPTER 28 — DAVID 100 MPH DRIVING

During Saul's visit from Connecticut in the summer of 1965, he and MacArthur went for a ride with David in his 1955 Buick Roadmaster. After having a few drinks, they got in the car to return home. David pushed the accelerator to the floor, and within seconds, the three were speeding along at 100 miles per hour. At first it was thrilling to ride at such a fast speed, MacArthur said, but when David failed to slow down at a deep snake curve, he and Saul became frightened and asked their brother to reduce his speed. He refused. MacArthur threatened to turn off the car ignition. David replied that he would turn the car over if he did. Still going 100 miles per hour, David took his hands off the steering wheel, only steering with one finger whenever the car pulled to the edge of the road. MacArthur said the cotton and cornfields were a blur. Suddenly he saw three white caskets side by side, holding his body, David's, and Saul's. MacArthur began to cry, wailing, "Lord, Lord, poor Mama done lost three of her sons." He began to pray for their safety. Saul, the wise one, knowing a fool was at the wheel, decided that the best course of action was to say nothing. It was a torturous ride, but he knew that if he got out alive, it would be the last time he rode with David at the wheel. After an eight-mile ride at 100 miles per hour, they arrived safely at Mama's home.

David got his driver's license at age fifteen. A few months later, on March 5, 1956, he raised his age to sixteen and successfully applied for a school bus driver position. David began driving a school bus in September of 1956. The summer of 1957, he quit school and began to work as a food server at a South Carolina mental institution, Crafts-Farrow. He later worked at Winnsboro Mills but returned to Crafts-Farrow, where he remained until his retirement June 30, 1991.

In February 1961, he met Lillie Davis Harrison, a young widow with three children. She also was a food service aide at Crafts-Farrow. After several months of courtship, they married on November 9, 1961. He became father to Christol, Walter, and Randy. His family soon expanded with the birth of Pamela, and then Carolyn Belton Brown, whose mother is Lucile Belton Martin.

David loved cars. During a ten-year period, he claimed he owned about forty cars. If you had the time to listen, he could describe each one in detail, as well as how it died. At first, Mama helped him by cosigning for the cars. She soon discovered this was costly, so she stopped. David, however, found other ways to continue his favorite hobby.

David was constantly cracking jokes. He could take a simple incident, poke fun at it, and turn it into a big, fun event. One such occasion was when he had a car accident late one night while riding with his buddy Stuffy. The car turned over a couple of times. Both doors sprung wide open and jammed so that the car resembled a small airplane. The car could not be driven. According to David, the radio was tuned to Randy's Records playing rock and roll music. As he and Stuffy waited along the dark highway, David began to dance. Stuffy joined him. After this performance, some called David "Zorba the Black Greek."

CHAPTER 29 — VISITING GRANDPA SAUL

In July 1978, my cousins and I returned to Longtown, South Carolina, to attend a birthday celebration for Grandpa Saul at the Stone family homestead. During this visit we recalled memories of Grandpa Saul and Grandma Ella hosting Thanksgiving dinners there every year, with family and friends from far and near gathering to celebrate. It was a joyous occasion.

I remembered a place full of life and nature at its best, but a quick observation revealed how much things had changed since my child-hood. The blooming flowers were gone. The chinaberry tree where we girls gathered to play and talk had lost its luster and was aging.

The house was worn and in need of repair. The smokehouse was still standing, in need of care, but with the lock still in place. Grandma Ella believed in keeping it locked. The smokehouse was where all the best meats and jars of canned foods were kept. It was full of goodies that children and grown-ups couldn't wait to sink their teeth into, such as sugar canned hams, smoked hams, bacon sides, canned pears, apples, peaches, string beans, and preserves.

I visited the garden where rutabaga, cabbage, onions, white pota-toes, sweet potatoes, and beets once grew abundantly. The space was filled with grass and weeds. I could not locate the spot where the pump once stood ready to supply fresh water. It was used to transmit water to the barn where the mules were kept.

I remembered a farm that had everything. Now there were no turkeys, chickens, geese, or hens. No cows, pigs, or horses. There were no sugar canes, no wheat, and no corn.

It was a sad feeling, reminiscing about the good times I had on the farm as a child. Times bring about a change, not just physically but emotionally. My cousins and I now were grown-ups with fat faces, fat behinds, and gray hairs beginning to play peek-a-boo. Many years had gone by since we had last met. We hugged, kissed, and often asked, "What's your name?"

CHAPTER 30 — FAMILY REUNIONS

Our family held its first reunion in 1986 at Mama's house in Ridgeway, South Carolina. Alberta and MacArthur initiated this idea. Family members were spread about, living in different parts of the country, including Washington, D.C., Connecticut, and Rhode Island, away from their roots. The reunion was a chance for relatives to bring their children, who otherwise had little opportunity to meet their aunts, uncles, and cousins. So began the tradition of a reunion to "stay connected to family on the vine," as Alberta put it. For seven years, the reunion was held yearly.

The second reunion also was in Ridgeway. For the third reunion, the family decided to gather in Norwich, Connecticut. A fish fry was held at Saul and Joyce's home. Saul and Freddie did the frying. Dorothy and Joyce made potato salad, coleslaw, and boiled sweet corn. Dinner was served country style. The next day family members went to Mohegan Park, where they enjoyed a catered meal.

Our fifth reunion, in 1990, was a memorable reunion at the Holiday Inn in Columbia, South Carolina, and fifty-seven family members and friends gathered. The air was filled with laughter as relatives exchanged greetings. All of the siblings were present with their families. Joining us were Mama's sisters Rosa and Nancy, Cousin Mattie and her family.

My grandchildren, Billy-Clyde and Lakeesha, and I attended through the generosity of Freddie, who drove us down. Freddie's wife, Dorothy, and their children rode in a separate car. I barely survived the drive in 106-degree heat. It was only 70 degrees when we left Connecticut, but blazing hot in South Carolina, with temperatures hovering around 100 degrees. I was drained, hot, and mean-spirited by the time we arrived. The children headed for the pool and the Jacuzzi.

The host family had planned a wonderful and interesting two days. On Saturday the group visited the state Capitol just ahead of the gay rights march. During dinner that evening, the entertainment included a fashion show. Natasha modeled, followed by her Grandpa Saul. Aunt Rosa showed the youngsters just how you are supposed to "strut" when modeling. Mattie gave a little wiggle as she modeled her finery, which met with lots of laughter. It surprised everyone except her husband. Angela, Shonne, James, and Darryl modeled formal wear. They were spectacular and lovely to look at. Eugene demonstrated his professional training in modeling.

The family reunion usually turns, taking on the flavor of a church meeting. First, greetings, hugs, handshakes, acknowledgements, and prayers, and then comes the member with one drink of courage to place matters in perspective or "ready to turn matters out." This particular year, Freddie said his piece and then some when he suggested the children dig deeper into their purses for their mother. It reminded me of the story of the minister who starts off the collection with twenty dollars, saying he has little but nevertheless is being generous, adding that there are others in the audiences who have been blessed by the Lord far more than he, and therefore he knows they will be generous and at least match his twenty dollars.

For the eighth reunion, in 1995, the family took in the rich history of Charleston, South Carolina, which emerged from the turmoil of the

American Revolution. To hear the click of the hooves of horses pulling carriages along the city's streets is to listen to the pace of life a century ago. The city is a living museum, with its gently tolling church bells, magnificent eighteenth-century homes, plantations, and spectacular gardens. There is an abundance of things to do, and family members enjoyed the sights.

This reunion also proved to be a reminder that the "black experience" of racism was alive and still practiced by whites in South Carolina. My grandson Billy Clyde and I arrived in Charleston by Amtrak the early morning of June 23, 1995. I left Billy Clyde, who was sixteen, with our luggage as I went to get transportation to our hotel. I returned to find him surrounded by four police officers demanding to search his bags. I was told they were doing a random check for drugs because people had been bringing drugs into Charleston. I believe a white young male accompanied by an adult dressed as we were would not have been searched. It was a humiliating experience for us.

Our ninth family reunion in 1997 was held at Water's Edge in Westbrook, Connecticut. The theme was "Let the Circle Not Be Broken." It had been two years since the untimely death of our sister Lillie. She was missed. This reunion was a memorable one because my siblings joined me in giving a training session called Survival Skills for Now and the Twenty-First Century. Topics included: employment issues; economic survival; and relationships, including marriage, family, work, and other issues that affect relationships. They were presented by Saul, MacArthur, Alberta, her husband Grant, and myself.

In 1999, our tenth family reunion was held in Fort Washington, Maryland. The topic for this reunion was centered on health and the benefits of organ donation. Freddie's wife, Dorothy Mae, had been the recipient of a donated kidney. This information later turned out to be helpful in making a decision following the unexpected death of Isiah, the son of Angela Dortch and Aaron Green, before the age of one due to a sunflower seed taking a wrong path. We cried and celebrated Isiah's life, and we were glad we'd had the discussion of organ donation.

Our last family reunion was in 2010 was held in Norwich, Connecticut, as a tribute to Freddie, who had become too sick to travel. He was Mama's helper when Daddy was unable to work. The family wanted to thank Freddie for his contributions and for his steadfastness in helping others.

Chapter 31 — Tribute To Mama On Her Seventy-Fifth Birthday

On July 3, 1992, the family gathered at the Purity Lodge in Ridgeway, South Carolina, in honor of Mama on her seventy-fifth birthday and this is the tribute I wrote for the occasion:

Seventy-five years is a long time—or a short time depending upon the context in which it is viewed. Seventy-five years is a short time when comparing it to the life of Methuselah. It is a long time when considering the life span of young black males. With so many people living to be 100 years old, it is the dawning of a golden era. Today, we join Estelle, our mother, sister, aunt, grandmother, great-grandmother, friend, and mentor in celebrating the commencement of a golden era.

Like Sojourner Truth, Mama could plow the fields, and like Harriet Tubman, she used a shotgun when necessary to protect her family and property, or to discourage intrusion. No celebration is complete without a reflection on the past. No journey should commence without first reviewing past journeys.

Mama was a pioneer in her own right long before it was considered all right for women to assert themselves on equal footing with men. She sought credit knowing that no one gave credit to women, and when she was told her husband needed to sign, her reply was, 'I am doing the work. What do you mean my husband must sign for me?'

She always had dreams beyond working on someone else's land and depending on others. Her favorite saying is, 'Mother may have, father may have, sister may have, brother may have, but God bless the child who has his own,' as sung by Billie Holiday in 1939. She did not subscribe to the opinion that you do nothing and just wait for your inheritance. She expressed the view that you work for what you want and depend on no one.

Mama dreamed of owning her home. This dream came true when she purchased her own home in Ridgeway. This house was not much to look at, but she said, 'It's mine.' She did not believe in working all your life and having nothing to show for your labors. Today, this 'dream' house, painted white with black shutters, and surrounded by beautiful flowering plants and vegetables, is beautiful. When she comes out the front door, as she looks to the right, she sees the residence of her grandson Dwayne Bell and his wife Hazel. When she walks around the back of the house, she comes face-to-face with the home of her son MacArthur, his wife Jessie Mae, and their youngest son, Darryl. Now she is witnessing her granddaughter Reecy and her husband John build their home across the street.

In seventy-five years, Mama has witnessed her children and grandchildren achieve goals that at one time were thought to be fool hearted for blacks. All eight children have been achievers, each in their own right and their own way. You will find a builder, a deacon, a mechanical tradesman, an attorney, a homemaker, an administrative worker, and a civil rights manager.

Mama was not satisfied with having eight children, many grandchildren, and great-grandchildren. She wanted more. So she adopted Mattie and Inell, and added another dozen or so to the family.

She is devoted to her sisters and brothers. She is willing to help when and however she can. Mama is known for her straight talk. She does not mince her words to make them more palatable to the listener or the target of her comments. After delivering her remarks, which often sting, she usually ends with, 'I don't mean no harm.'

As most of her children have reached the half-century mark, they are beginning to seek her advice on many things, but mostly on how to keep healthy. They are asking her to share old home remedies. The more they learn from reading their books, the more they realize how much Mama knows—and knew long before it was printed in the books. She has taught that common sense prevails, and it can take you farther than formal education.

Today is a joyous time, as family members and friends join Mama on the occasion of her seventy-fifth birthday. To her we say, 'Our lives have been enriched by your love, devotion, understanding, straight talk, and being there for us in time of need. We wish you good health and happiness as you begin your golden years. Happy seventy-fifth birthday!'

Chapter 32 — Visits With The Aunts

In 2012, I went with Clifford, my friend and companion, to Atlanta, Georgia. After spending a couple of days there to celebrate his brother's seventy-fifth birthday, then a couple of days in Myrtle Beach, we were off to visit where I grew up in Longtown, South Carolina. I began to make my rounds of visits where I was always greeted warmly, and with a lot of food and remembrances of childhood.

Aunt Baby Ruth was ready for my visit. She had fried chicken, fried fish, collards cooked with smoked turkey necks, butter beans cooked with fatback, and corn bread cooked in a black cast iron skillet to perfection—with a deep brownish top and a thick bottom crust. Of course, string beans were cooked with fatback. A fresh-baked coconut pie sat on the side table, along with a sweet potato pie and pound cake. Also, sweet tea—I mean real sweet with real sugar.

Aunt Baby Ruth was concerned she had not prepared enough food for me and offered to pull out of the freezer a couple of squirrels to make a stew. I began to salivate as I remembered how delicious squirrel tasted during my childhood years. Clifford raised his voice, looking directly at me: "Rabies!" Aunt Baby Ruth looked at Clifford in sheer astonishment. "You have rabies in Connecticut?" Clifford replied, "Rabies is everywhere." Aunt Baby Ruth replied, "Oh, no, not here." I declined the offer of squirrel stew not because of rabies, but because the quiet lion had roared.

As we prepared to leave, Aunt Baby Ruth began to fill two takeout containers with food. "No, no," I said. Her reply: "I cannot eat this food. I have diabetes, high blood pressure, high cholesterol, and heart trouble. My doctor says I should eat this kind of food only once in a while. My faith in God keeps me strong. Every morning, I pray and talk with God. I listen to His Word," as she passed the containers to me.

A long-standing tradition in our family during visits to Longtown was to see as many family members as possible. I didn't visit South Carolina very much in the early years after moving to Connecticut, but I began yearly visits in the late 1990s. I would stop by to visit Uncle JB and Aunt Dinah, along with Uncle McKinley and Aunt Baby Ruth. After Uncle McKinley's accidental death on August 4, 1999, I began to spend more time with Aunt Baby Ruth. I always left bearing jars of fig preserves, and coconut pies made with lots of coconut, butter, sugar and her special pie crust. No one made coconut pies like Aunt Baby Ruth.

On this particular occasion, as we entered Aunt Baby Ruth's home, we were greeted by the aroma of fried chicken, fried fish, lima beans, pig feet, and catfish stew. My childhood memories returned in full gear. Something special peered at me from beneath a lid. The aroma I couldn't identify, but sliding the lid just a little showed thick brown gravy covering something underneath. As I peered at the brown gravy, wondering what it could be covering, Aunt Baby Ruth said it was a rabbit that had been caught a couple of days ago. The thought of eating young, tender rabbit made my mouth water. Aunt Baby Ruth wasted no time passing a plate to me and proceeded to fill it. I quickly devoured the food and licked clean the plate!

Oh, how I remembered the joy of eating rabbit as a child. I recall seeing the little brown rabbits running and playing in a large green space near the Connecticut Department of Motor Vehicles office in Norwich, Connecticut. As they ran about freely, I wished for a slingshot to "cream" one and take it home. In truth, even if I'd had a slingshot, I wouldn't have used it, for fear I would be dragged off to jail and charged with animal cruelty. Then I traveled back in time, remembering Mama saying so often that "white folks just had such fool notions about things." Yelp!

During my visits to South Carolina, Aunt Dinah and Uncle JB were a must-stop. If it was during Thanksgiving, we would travel to have dinner at the Stone homestead. It was an opportunity to meet cousins who maybe were visiting from Detroit, Florida, or New York. Aunt Dinah always prepared a delicious meal.

Most children in Longtown learn at an early age that they have many cousins. Most of the time, the connection on how they became cousins is not explained. Once you become a teenager and begin to take an interest in the opposite sex, you learn that every boy or girl who wishes to begin a courtship is a relative. Then an adult will announce that everyone is related and proclaim that the Belton's are related to everyone. You have double cousins, aunts, and uncles.

One day I discovered that my cousin Dinah had become my aunt. I had to stop calling her Dinah and begin calling her Aunt Dinah. This came about when Mama's brother, James Benjamin Stone, called JB, married Dinah Bell, who is the daughter of Daddy's brother Albert and Lallie Outten Bell. This made Dinah a first cousin, and an aunt. She never let me forget that she was my aunt, and cousin. Respect required that I call her Aunt Dinah.

Uncle JB met Aunt Dinah, who was thirteen at the time, at Mount Olive Baptist Church and announced to her that she was going to be his wife. Shortly thereafter, he enlisted in the U.S. Navy and was honorable discharged in December 1945. Upon his return to civilian life,

Uncle JB began a hot pursuit of his love interest. Their courtship was the talk of Longtown, South Carolina. All eyes were upon them as they walked hand in hand to and from church. At times, Uncle JB would place an arm around her waist, but his hand would inch slowly upward until it landed just beneath her breast line. People watched but did not say a "mumbling word." Their courtship was short. Uncle JB and Aunt Dinah married April 11, 1946, four months after they began dating. Aunt Dinah was a month short of her sixteenth birthday. Soon two sons, Israel and James, joined them. It was not long before the grand- and great-grandchildren came.

During my visits with Aunt Geneva, the wife of Daddy's brother George, she always gave me a tour of her gallery of photos featuring their children, grandchildren, great-grandchildren, and great-great-grandchildren. She did not call their names but introduced them thus: "This here is my doctor, and this is my other doctor. Here is my nurse. This one delivers babies. This here one, she traveled overseas to help poor people." Then Aunt Geneva does an Estelle Bell: she begins to adopt. "Here is my attorney. This here is my other attorney." She is proud to be greeted by a young man who is a local funeral director. His mother grew up in the neighborhood along with our families. Aunt Geneva is proud to be a helper caring for the children while their parents and grandparents worked. She reads to the children and tells them they are smart.

During one of my visits with Aunt Geneva, I had with me an obituary of her mother, Marie Goins Butler, which I had read. When I inquired about the name Goins, she simply said, "Old Man George Goins is my granddaddy." I was shocked! Her mother and my Grandma Ella were sisters, making her an aunt and a cousin.

During the early days of their marriage, Uncle George and Aunt Geneva lived with Grandpa Joe and Cuzin Julia. When Grandpa Joe purchased property near Kershaw County, he moved there along with Cuzin Julia and Aunt Della's three children, Joseph, Blanche, and Randolph. Their mother had to leave the children because of spousal abuse. Uncle George and Aunt Geneva moved into the older home. They had twelve children.

All farmers in the surrounding neighborhood area worked hard whether sharecropping or working the land of a family member. The old saying "you reap what you sow" was very appropriate. If the farmers did not plant well, till often, and protect their crops, they and their children would lack shoes and many other items of necessity. Uncle George and Aunt Geneva had more children than other nearby families.

Most parents had limited education. Farm work took priority over homework. When children stayed out of school often to help with farming, usually it was when they reached their teens.

Without moving north, the only jobs available were pulpwood for young black men and next to nothing for young women. Parents knew the importance of education and wanted a better life for their children. So when an opportunity became available for the twins, Martha and Mary, to move to Washington, D.C., Aunt Geneva and Uncle George agreed that Martha could go live with Uncle Philip and Aunt Lucretia. A year later, Mary went to live with Uncle Moses and Aunt Mary Alice. Soon, Norvice, the fourth-oldest child, moved to Connecticut to assist me with childcare. Aunt Geneva says she has no regrets about letting her children leave, because they would have had a hard life had they stayed. Moving gave them benefits not available on the farm, and in turn they could open doors of opportunity for their children.

Uncle George set his sights on a marriage between his son George Jr. and Mary Frances, a neighbor's daughter. The two were not even teens when Uncle George deemed that this union would take place, and it did. Uncle George was smitten by the girl's fair skin and long blond hair.

Aunt Geneva dressed beautifully and looked twenty years younger than her age. At her one-hundredth birthday celebration, everyone adopted her and called her Mother. She had taken to going on cruises; she loved to travel and did not fear going out to sea.

Lottie Mae Griffin Russell and I visited our cousin Nancy Belton Ross Jackson. We both had had a lifelong relationship with Nancy, whom most people called by her nickname, Dossier. She was the daughter of George Belton Jr. and Candace Law Tucker. It was common knowledge that Great-Grandpa George had children outside of his marriage but had no children with his second wife, Mary Alice Slater Belton, who was called Missy.

At the age of five, Nancy was badly burned. When she lifted her dress to take the lid off a pot cooking over the fire coals, her dress caught fire. Someone patted the dress trying to put out the fire. Her father pulled the dress over her head, and she was burned from her neck to the bottom of her abdomen. Dr. Dobson came to the house to treat her and gave her a lemon-colored oil for application to the wound. During her recovery, Nancy was cared for at home by her cousins, who fanned her to keep flies away from the wound. She married and gave birth to seven boys. She said she had difficulties during pregnancy because her body was unable to stretch. Nancy said that doctors who cared for her over the years were amazed she had survived. She said God is a healer and all things are possible. She then abruptly lifted her dress and showed the scars left by the burn.

Nancy recollects that she lived well while staying at her grandfather's house. It was beautifully furnished. There was an organ that was played daily by his wife, her Aunt Missy. Nancy said there was never a want for food or clothing. The family members dressed very well. She said Grandfather George owned many acres of land, as far as the eye could see, near the Wateree River. He was a blacksmith and a bootlegger, and worked a farm as well. There were rumors aplenty that Aunt Missy was one mean woman and did not like George's children, but Cousin Nancy says Aunt Missy was good to her.

CHAPTER 33 — THANKSGIVING TRADITIONS CONTINUE

November 24, 1989 was a sunny, clear, and mild day. Family members gathered at Mama's home in Ridgeway to celebrate Thanksgiving. Alberta and Josephine took to the kitchen to prepare dinner. The menu included roast turkey, corn bread dressing, chitterlings, honey baked ham, green beans, garden salad, potato salad, fruit salad, rice salad, cranberry sauce, punch, corn bread, and muffins. Desserts were sweet potato pies, coconut pies, thirty-day cake, plain pound cake, and coconut layer cake. A circle was formed: hands held around the table. Grant Williams said grace. Josephine asked each individual to share his or her reason for being thankful. Alberta expressed her thankfulness for our family, but also for having Michelle with us. She had traveled from California to be with family. Michelle thanked everyone for their prayers. She told us she was doing well, and we could stop worrying. Michelle passed on July 23, 1990, at the age of twenty-one.

• • •

It was Wednesday, November 25, 1998, and Clifford and I had traveled to South Carolina to be with family for Thanksgiving. It was also an opportunity to see my former classmates from Fairfield County Training School. We went to Winnsboro to shop for food. Mama said she could not go with us because she had been out the day before; she could only go out every other day. We spent several hours in Winnsboro. We drove to the site of my alma mater, Fairfield County Training School. It now seemed so very small. More than forty-five years before, it seemed huge. Perhaps it was the perception of a country girl.

Mariah Jackson, owner of a local grocery store, was still operating, and her brother was the clerk. This little store was the hangout for high school students. Those of us who rode the bus twenty-four miles to get to school would on rare occasions arrive early for the opportunity to go to the store before the class bell rang. We ate candy, drank Dr Pepper and Pepsi, and danced to the latest record. I watched with amazement as the students danced to "Work with Me, Annie," "Annie Had a Baby," and many more. Parents thought the music was shameful. I did not pay attention to the words, as I was intrigued by the dancing.

Returning to the high school brought back many memories. Mrs. Charleton, the wife of the principal, was very nice to me. When I had a stress attack, she took me out on the front steps of the school to get fresh air. Mr. Charleton came by and made a smart remark about my being there. He disapproved. She disapproved of his rudeness. Mrs. Charleton was a very kind and sweet person. Her husband was just the opposite.

Fairfield County Training School holds fond memories as well as painful ones. Being poor and not well dressed were negatives. You stood out because of your humble condition. No one was seeking you out for friendship. The handsome, well-dressed boys sought the well-dressed, attractive girls who had coordinated clothes and wore the latest style.

Those of us from the country wore simple clothing, our socks splashed by mud puddles or dingy from too many hand washings.

• • •

Thanksgiving dinner 2005 was held in Columbia, South Carolina, at the home of Josephine and Joey Patton. Dinner was fabulous. The baby girl who had burned Mama's food in her high school years was at her best. The menu included roast turkey, Cajun and smoked roasted ham, roasted pork, corn bread dressing, macaroni and cheese, gravy, potato salad, turnip greens, green beans, rolls, and cranberry sauce. Dessert was sweet potato pies, pumpkin pies, and cakes. There were a few different flavors of pound cake—Mama's favorite. Clifford said he did not like sweet potato pie, but changed his tune upon a bite of Mama's.

After dinner, Darlene, Darryl, and their daughters, Jordin, age five, and Erica, age three, came by for a visit, along with MacArthur and his son Dwayne. MacArthur did not recognize me because of Alzheimer's disease. Jordin and Erica enjoyed seeing "Big Mama Estelle," whom they clearly missed since she had moved to Columbia with Joey and Josephine. It was beautiful watching their expressions and listening to the conversation between Mama and her great-grandchildren. Jordin and Erica would ask questions and Mama answered them in a language they understood. Their voices were calm, sweet, and loving. Jordin rubbed the dog Grace's stomach as she rolled on her back. "She really loves me," Jordin cooed.

MacArthur and Mama were so happy to be together. They sat holding hands tightly, Mama saying over and over again, "My son, my son," and MacArthur smiling broadly. It was a tender moment. Both were suffering from Alzheimer's disease but still holding on to their strong love for each other.

Chapter 34 — A Tribute
To Our Ancestors In 2008

In 2008, the Bell family reunion was held in Columbia, South Carolina and coincided with Mama's ninetieth birthday. I designed and led the family on a journey of ancestors' grounds. We visited their birthplaces, where they lived, worked, worshipped, died, and were buried. This is history that we do not want to lose. Graves are used today all over America to help families tell their family history.

Town of Ridgeway, South Carolina
Ridgeway was a very special place to be on Saturday. This is the place people went to sell their cotton, shop for needed goods, pay their debt to the merchants, and socialize with friends. There was an impressive loading dock for holding cotton bales until it was time to load onto railroad cars for transporting to manufacturing factories. A large cotton gin mill was used for removing seeds from the cotton before packing it into bales.

Stop 1: Longtown, South Carolina
This was the birthplace of our parents and their children. Mama and

Daddy's house stood about a mile from a main crossroad marked by the Reeves Country Store. The store remains today and is adjacent to the Windmill Restaurant. At the time, it was owned by Thomas Reeves. It was the only store nearby. The next place to buy supplies and food was in Ridgeway, about eleven miles away, and families nearby depended on Mr. Reeves's store. By springtime, most families had used up all their cash, and they had to rely upon purchasing food and supplies on credit. They were extended credit to purchase food and supplies until harvest time. When harvest time came and they paid their debts, they had barely enough money left to purchase clothes and food staples for their families.

The store was a place where men and young boys gathered on a Saturday afternoon after taking their weekly bath and putting on their starched overalls. At the Reeves' store, they sat on kegs, drinking Pepsi and playing cards. They would sneak a little moonshine and hold lying contests.

Mary Reeves, wife of Thom Reeves, was rude, hateful, and disrespectful. When giving change, she would not always give the correct amount. Daddy was her match. He could add and subtract and count money.

Many years later, Uncle Albert Bell and his wife Lallie Bell purchased the Reeves' home. During a visit, Aunt Lallie Bell and I sat on the porch recalling Mary Reeves and her treatment of black people. We clapped our hands and laughed with delight. Aunt Lallie Bell said, "I wonder what Miss Mary Reeves is doing and feeling, now that black people are living in this house."

Stop 2: Homestead of Solomon and Ella Stone
Ella and Solomon Stone purchased land and a home under a special governmental farm program. David Belton, a cousin, worked with Solomon Stone on securing the program. A model farm of that day was

developed: white, three bedrooms, with a porch, a pantry, a smoke-house, an outhouse, chicken coops, a modern barn for livestock, and a pumping system to provide water inside the home and a watering place for the animals.

On Thanksgiving Day, our grandparents hosted a dinner for family members. All the children, grandchildren, cousins, uncles, aunts, brothers, and sisters came. The aunts were known for their baking skills, and made all kinds of cakes and pies. Children were not allowed in the kitchen. The men took off to the woods to hunt, returning with rabbits and coons. Sometimes Grandpa Saul would butcher a calf for the event. Our grandparents raised chickens, cattle, hogs, turkey, and sugar cane from which molasses was made. There was corn, white and sweet potatoes, all types of vegetables, grapes, and fruit trees. Grandma Ella canned fruits and meats. Her pantry was never bare, nor was the smokehouse. Food seemed to be plentiful all year long.

Stop 3: Mount Joshua Church
Our paternal great-grandparents Warren Bell and Nora Roach were buried here, as well as Daddy's parents, Joe Bell Sr. and Dinah Belton Bell. Also laid to rest are Daddy's sister Mary Alice Benson and her husband, as well as other relatives.

Stop 4: Homestead of Charity Kirkland Goins and George Goins
Our maternal great-grandparents Charity Kirkland Goins and George Goins lived in Kershaw County. Charity Kirkland's parents were Sally Green and Chapman Kirkland. Our grandmother Ella Goins Stone was one of many children of the couple. Charity became blind at a young age. I remember her visit as a young child. Grandma Charity used her hand to feel the contour of my face and hair, and announced that I was pretty but should pin my long hair close to my head. She warned me to

watch out during a fight because a person could wrap my hair around their hand and hurt me.

Across the highway, opposite the Kirkland site, was Mr. White's store, which was a very popular hangout. Mr. White married Grandpa Joe's sister, Nicky Bell, the youngest child of Nora and Warren Bell. It was said that everyone in Fairfield County was related. The White, Bell, Roach, Goins, and Kirkland families were deeply intertwined by blood and marriage. Generations of Bell, Belton, Roach, Stone, Goins, Tucker, and Kirkland all have some family ties because of living in close proximity. This is believed to have happened because of limited mobility of traveling outside of their counties in South Carolina.

Stop 5: Rock Hill Baptist Church

Among the relatives buried at this site are Charity and George Goins Sr. and their son who died as a young adult. Our paternal great-grandfather George Belton, born 1861 and died early 1935, and at least one of his wives were said to be buried here also. Some relatives are very specific about the location, saying it was near a small tree. However, no grave marker has been found for either of them at Rock Hill or Mount Olive. There are markers for our great-great-grandfather George Belton, born 1830 and died 1886, and his wife Amanda, born 1832 and died 1888.

Stop 6: Second house of Joe Bell Sr.

Grandpa Joe moved here after trading property with white landowner Mr. Kirkland for some of the land he owned at his original home in Fairfield County near the Wateree River. When he moved, his son George moved with his family into the old home site. Grandpa Joe could not read or write. He did his own negotiations. It was whispered that Mr. Kirkland was taking advantage of Grandpa. The two men would meet, drink moonshine, talk, and walk the property. Sometimes this would go on for days and nights. Over time the two men reached an agreement. There was never a dispute between the two about land boundaries.

Grandpa Joe's common-law wife Cuzin Julia had her money pouch to spend as she chose. Grandpa was never heard telling her what to do with her money. If someone needed a loan, Cuzin Julia would lend money, and she expected to be repaid. Looking back, she was "her own woman." Grandpa did not control her, and no one ever heard her intervene in or criticize how Grandpa handled his relationships with others.

Stop 7: Antioch Baptist Church, Old Cemetery

The church was completed in 1883. This is the burial site of Solomon and Ella Goins Stone, Great-Grandfather William Stone and his wife Janie Derry Stone, as well as some of their children: King Solomon Stone and his wife Etta Tucker Stone; Scillar Stone Loynes and her husband Major; Samuel Stone; Eli Stone; Mary Stone, wife of Prince Jesse Stone; and Laura Ruth Stone.

This site had a small white church. During the summer, many dinners were held at noon to accommodate members who wanted to attend afternoon or evening church services. Most had to walk, travel by wagon, or ride their mules or horses to get to church. Few people had cars during the early years.

Baptism was done in a local water hole across from the church. "Wade in the Water" was sung during the baptism ceremony. This type of ceremony inspired many artists in creating their work. Alvin Ailey's *Revelations* is one example.

Our grandparents Solomon and Ella Stone were very involved in the church. Solomon was a deacon for many years, and taught Sunday school until he was in his early 90s. Ella and Sarah were sisters who married two brothers: Solomon and Benjamin. Benjamin also served as a deacon for many years. The Stones were the movers and shakers in the church, and the family's presence remains strong today.

Benjamin and Solomon's parents were buried on the grounds of Antioch. Their children were active in the church. Uncle McKinley served as a deacon until his death. Vera, his daughter, is now an associate minister at Rock Hill Baptist Church.

In 1963, the congregation built a new church on Old Windmill Road, a short distance from the former building, which is now a burial ground. The family continues to be involved in the church. Major Jr. and Elijah, sons of Scillar Stone Loynes and Major Loynes, Sr. are active in the church.

Stop 8: Mount Olive Baptist Church

The first service was held under the brush arbor on a Sunday in May of 1885. One year later the brush arbor began to leak, so the group decided to build a house to worship in. The people called it "Sunday School and Prayer House." Buried at this site are our father, mother, sister Lillie, brother Saul, Daddy's brothers George and Albert, and many from the Bell and Belton families. The Bell descendants still attend the church. Dwayne and Moses are Deacons. Reecy has chosen to attend Rock Hill, along with her mother, where her grandparents were pillars.

After many generations, Mount Olive, Antioch, and Rock Hill Churches are still predominantly served by children of our ancestors. Growing up, my brothers and I were fearful of being near a cemetery. The younger generation was joyful and playful there. Someone said the children would never forget the experience of the tour.

The tour was done nearly ten years ago. A lot of change has occurred in our lives, but the ancestors' churches are still vibrant and the center of family. The traditions of our ancestors continue in the lives of their descendants.

REFLECTIONS

REFLECTIONS

CHAPTER 35 — MISS M.

The Reeves Country Store owned by Thomas Reeves and his wife Mary, whom we called Miss M. The country store was close by and very important to the farmers in Longtown. This was where they purchased supplies and food for the family year round. Mr. Reeves was a pleasant man but his wife was rude and mean. Miss M. knew that most of the farmers did not have a good education and she took advantage of that when it came to purchasing or selling supplies. At times, Miss M. gave more money to the person than was due. No one would point out her error, and no one called it dishonesty. She was getting back what she sowed.

For Mama and Daddy, reading, writing, and math were not good. Daddy was great at counting money but not at multiplying. Math skills were very important. It was the general feeling of our parents and others that some white merchants were quick to take advantage of black farmers who did not read well. So Mama and Daddy would ask me to add up all their debts before taking their cotton bales to the merchants to sell. The amount of the debt would be subtracted from the amount the merchant paid for the cotton. A bale of cotton could weigh 200 pounds or 250 pounds after seeds were removed. It could sell for 32 cents, more or less, per pound, depending upon the quality of the cotton. So before Daddy left home, he and I would figure out several possibilities on the amount of money he should receive. His memory was keen, and no one could cheat him out of a penny once he knew how much money he was entitled to receive. Daddy had no problem letting merchants know that he had a smart daughter.

Miss M. would pretend she accidentally dropped a black person's change between the candy jars where you could not reach it. She would not offer to get the change but would give the person a "daring you" look to put their hand on the jars. So they did not.

Miss M. was bound and determined to cheat Daddy, but he was too fast for her. One day he came home grinning from ear to ear. Mama asked him why the grinning. He said that Miss M. was so busy trying to cheat him out of money that she cheated herself. Mama and Daddy had a great laugh, and no one called it being dishonest. The word went out "Old Miss M." was not just mean and spiteful, but dumb.

In 1956 when I was about eight months pregnant, Miss M. purposely threw my change on the floor and stood there watching with a sardonic grin on her face as I struggled to retrieve it. Miss M. fed her little white dogs steak cut into bite-sized pieces in front of the store where all could see, and she would be grinning ear to ear as if to say, "You wish you had this to eat." She knew we were poor and had little to eat at times. The message: Dogs' lives were valued over the lives of black folks. So I began to hate Miss M. and her dogs. In fact, all the pretty little dogs that rode in the front seats of their white owners' cars.

On a Saturday evening when the black men gathered at the store to socialize, Miss M. would go home every few minutes to change clothes. She would just be grinning and switching her butt when passing them as she went back and forth from her house to the store. The men knew to keep their heads down. The women had warned their men not to make eye contact with her, while all the time keeping an eye on

Miss M. There was no telling what she may do. Her husband was a nice man in that he was pleasant in his dealing with blacks.

Witnessing Miss M.'s treatment of blacks, the beating of my cousin by the police, and other biased actions made it difficult for me to be forgiving when it came to white people. During my early years in Connecticut, however, I learned that holding on to ill feelings about former treatment only hurts you. I reasoned that no one knows about your feelings, and if they did, they would not care. This revelation helped me chart my course for dealing with injustices.

CHAPTER 36 — MISS M.'S HOUSE SOLD

During my trips to Longtown, I always visited Aunt Lallie Bell and Uncle Albert. On one occasion, I was surprised to learn they had just purchased the former home of Thomas and Mary Reeves. Aunt Lallie Bell invited me to join her on the front porch. We each plopped down in a rocking chair and soon began to reminisce about the bygone days in Longtown. We never dreamed that black folks would someday be sitting on the front porch of a home once owned by white people. The two of us began clapping our hands joyfully as we sat enjoying the beautiful surroundings of flowers, trees of every size, and green hue. In days gone by, black people did not dare walk on the same side of the road where the house stood. Now they were sitting on the front porch in rocking chairs, just rocking back and forth, and just a-clapping their hands. Aunt Lallie Bell and I could not stop laughing as we began to offer our opinions of where Miss M. was residing and how furious she must be.

Mama taught us that "trouble does not last always. The sun will shine in your back door someday. Just put God in front of you and the Devil behind you."

LIFE TRANSITIONS

CHAPTER 37 — DADDY GOES HOME

The hospital called to tell me that Daddy probably would not live through the night. I rushed to the hospital to be by his side. I found him breathing heavily and in a seemingly deep sleep. He did not respond to my call or touch. When I failed to get a response from him, I recalled the stormy relationship between the two of us. I said to myself, "Daddy won't use his last breath to acknowledge me. He is going to wait for Alberta and Freddie."

I rushed to a pay phone in the hospital lobby to call Alberta, who lived in Bradford, Rhode Island. Next I called David in South Carolina. Then I called Henry Randall, vice president of NAACP Norwich Branch, to have dinner. I wanted to take care of branch business and prepare him to take over during my absence to attend Daddy's funeral.

Alberta rushed to Daddy's bedside, placed his hand in hers, and called his name. She told him she was with him and that Freddie was on his way. Alberta continued to talk with him, and as Freddie walked into the room, she said, "Daddy, Freddie is here." Then Daddy took his last breath.

Daddy had been ill for several years and had grown increasingly weak during the last year. A heavy smoker all his life, he was suffering from emphysema. He knew he would die soon. Daddy's wish was to be returned to South Carolina and to be buried at Mount Olive Baptist Church, where he had held membership since he was a child. Daddy had chosen a black suit, pale pink shirt, black hat, and pink tie for his going away. He wanted a casket to complement his suit. He asked me to go to the funeral home to pick one for him.

After reviewing many caskets, I spotted one I liked and, without asking the price, said my father would love it. It was available and within Daddy's budget.

When I returned from the funeral home, Daddy asked for every minute detail about all the caskets, and a pleasant look came across his face when I described the cream-colored casket with a faint brocade design. It looked rich, I told him, and cost several times less than the quoted price. He was pleased.

Daddy had been a handsome man, but his illness had left him pale and thin. He also was hurt that his many friends had ceased visiting him. He instructed me to allow only family and devoted friends to view his body. I honored his request. However, when Daddy's body arrived in South Carolina, I was told to "step out of the way" since his wife was still alive. David and Mama took over and allowed a public viewing and photo taking of Daddy's body. I cried.

Daddy was born on August 4, 1912, and died on May 12, 1977.

A few years later, I received a telephone call from a young woman who introduced herself as Patricia, saying, "I am your sister." That is when I learned that Daddy had fathered two other children: Patricia and Joseph, during his separation from Mama when he moved up North to Norwich. Upon learning of this information, it was revealed to me that this was not a secret and my young nieces and nephews living in Norwich knew about them. Also, I found out Daddy had confided in MacArthur that he had fathered two children. Over the past forty years, contact with Patricia and Joseph has been minimal.

CHAPTER 38 — BEGINNING OF A FAMILY NIGHTMARE, SUMMER OF 1995

Our arrival in Charleston, South Carolina, for the family reunion in 1995 was marred by our treatment by police at the train station. They surrounded my grandson, asked to check his bags, and threatened to take him to jail if I did not allow this. I was afraid to let my grandson out of my sight, so I agreed to the search. I recalled the time in Ridgeway that I witnessed my cousin being beaten. I was less than twelve years old. My cousin was just talking to me when two white policemen walked up and, without saying anything, began beating him across the head with their sticks. They knocked him to the ground and dragged him up the street, kicking him all the way as they took him to the police station. I was horrified and never forgot that experience. As a child, I listened to the adults' whispers of how black men were beaten and dragged behind a pickup truck until they were dead. No, I did not want my grandson to be taken by the police. After the incident, we checked into our hotel, and I spent the day crying and seeking some authority to report the incident.

In the evening, I joined the family for a celebration of our being together. We took tours of Charleston to see the mansions and the slave dwellings. We enjoyed a boat ride. The days were filled with activities and chatting. Everyone learned that Alberta and Grant would soon welcome another grandchild. They would each have a grandchild to carry in their arms once Candice arrived and joined Chelah.

We departed Charleston and stopped in Longtown, South Carolina, to visit family in Ridgeway. We then left for Virginia, joining other family members, including Lillie, to attend the wedding of Terri and Darrin. There we danced and had lots of fun.

Shortly thereafter, I joined my friend Thomasina for a vacation in the Berkshires in Massachusetts. Saul and Joyce were basking in the joy of Terri's marriage. Meanwhile, Alberta was troubled by dreams of Lillie being surrounded by shootings. She told Grant of her dreams, which she did not understand. Lillie never went to bars or places where there would likely be trouble.

On August 4, we heard the unbelievable news that Lillie and two others had been killed by a gunman while working at McDonald's in Washington, D.C. I said Alberta had a gift of seeing and feeling what others did not. It was the beginning of a nightmare for our family.

Chapter 39 — Lillie's Killer Is Sentenced!

On January 11, 1997, Kenneth Joel Marshall plead guilty to two counts of felony murder and one count of second-degree murder for killing three co-workers at a McDonald's in Washington, D.C., including my sister Lillie. What follows is my letter to the court before his sentencing:

March 17, 1997

To the Honorable Mary Ellen Abrecht, in the matter of the death of Lillian Blondell Jackson caused by Kenneth Marshall:

On Friday, August 4, 1995, I was vacationing in the Berkshires with my friend, Thomasina. As we prepared to return home and spend a carefree day shopping along the way, I received the most devastating news: My sister Lillian Jackson had been killed with two employees while at work at McDonald's. Words are inadequate to express the shock and hurt I felt.

When I called my sister's twelve-year-old daughter, Marilyn LaTavia Jackson, the only words that came out were, "I love you, I love you." We both broke down and cried. What else could I say about her mother? During the next few days, I was in a state of trauma trying to cope and be helpful to other family members. Another memorable and painful time was the drive to South Carolina for the funeral. We all gathered at a gas station to fill our cars with gas for the long journey. Our brother-in-law, Grant Williams, asked us all, including the toddlers, to join hands, and with heavy hearts, we prayed for a safe journey for ourselves and those who would follow. It was a very, very sad occasion. My silent tears were nonstop for our seven-or-more-hour trip. But the worst came when I saw my mother, a woman who is known for her vitality and the happiness she exudes when her children come home. She had aged beyond her years, a once-upright body was stooped, and her eyes were red from crying. The home that was always filled with jubilation upon my arrival and the arrival of any one of the children was as silent as a tomb. My mother opened her arms to receive each of her remaining seven children as they walked through the door, one by one. No word was passed. The hurt was too deep for words. It was hurting for me to know that there was one child my mother would never again feel in her arms. Mama knew it too. Words are inadequate to express a hurt that is so penetrating and consuming, a hurt that was caused by a selfish and criminal act.

Mr. Kenneth Marshall took away from our family a loving and kind sister who always wore a cheerful smile. She had nothing ill to say about anyone and never got into any squabbles. During family gatherings, she always came with her husband John and three children. When the boys went out on their own, you could always count on Lillian, John, and Marilyn LaTavia showing up to whatever family event was taking place.

Mr. Marshall deserves the maximum sentencing under law and should not be eligible for parole during his lifetime. While nothing can bring back my sister Lillian, Your Honor, you can send a powerful message that murdering another person is not only against the law, but anyone committing such a crime will be punished and placed in a position where the opportunity to kill again will be greatly minimized.

I thank you for an opportunity to express to the court the impact that Lillian's death has had personally on me.

In Loving Memory of our Sister, Lillian Blondell Bell Jackson.

Lottie Mae Bell Scott

Marshall received eighty years in prison.

CHAPTER 40 — MEMORIES OF LILLIE BY HER CHILDREN

What follows are favorite memories of Lillie as shared by her three children.

Lillian Blondell Jackson married John L. Jackson in the summer of 1964, and had their first child, Thomas Pernell, on February 7, 1965. They later moved to Washington, D.C., where she became a home-maker—a great one—and three years later she had her second child, John Derwin, on April 4, 1968, the same day Dr. Martin Luther King Jr. was assassinated. It was a mess. Daddy was running around with his head cut off trying to get Mama to the hospital, and all the while she kept asking about the well-being of her firstborn son Thomas.

Mama began to raise her children and focused on her family. She thought she was finished with bearing children, but God had something in store for her. Fourteen years later she gave birth to a little girl on November 15, 1981. They named her Marilyn L. Jackson. Mama and Daddy were shocked upon learning of the pregnancy. All was well, as Daddy always wanted a little girl.

Mama always kept a smile on her face in spite of the situation. After she raised her two boys, she continued to raise her little girl along with her first grandchild Darrell. She was so proud of becoming a grandmother. Then she sent both of us off to school. Then here comes Marcus and Maranda. Mama loved to care for her grandchildren along with her nieces and nephews and cook homemade biscuits and sweet potato pies for us.

My mother had a smile that lit up a room that I will never forget. After she got us up to an age where she felt comfortable leaving us alone for a little while, she began to work at McDonald's restaurant. She was very dedicated as a store manager for ten years. Mama was a very dedicated person and always giving of herself. She never had a negative thing to say.

Mama was a wonderful and devoted wife to our father, a loving mother and grandmother. She was an active member at Mount Calvary Baptist Church and served on the usher board. Her life revolved around her family. She was gentle, loving, and kindhearted, but don't get her wrong, she would tear you up into pieces if you "angered her spirit."

I recall an incident with me. She had put some things on layaway, and the store had lost her order. Mama started crying. I asked her why. She told me that people had lost her order, and she could not get her money back. Also I would only get a winter coat for Christmas. I started crying, the spoiled child that I had become, and threw the coat on the floor. Within a flash, Mama slapped me, saying, "You pick up that coat or somebody will be picking you up. Can't get my money back, so," she said to me, "you can only get a winter coat." I started crying, being the spoiled child that I was. Oh, she was rough when she got angry. Some people think my father did all the discipline. No way. It was her.

Many people thought Mama didn't achieve anything in life, but they are wrong. She left behind three strong children that she and my father raised to the best of their ability. We have never been in any kind of trouble. I think they did a wonderful job, and I thank and praise God for that. Mama has five grandchildren—two of them biological she did not have the opportunity to have seen (my children) and three additional grandchildren by marriage—and I know she is looking down on us, smiling as usual.

— Marilyn LaTavia Jackson

I remember the good cooking; the homemade biscuits that Thomas seemed to have stolen from Mom; the sweet potato pies; chocolate/pineapple cakes. I also remember the strange things Mom use to cook to keep Dad happy. I remember one morning we were eating breakfast and Mom had scrambled some hog brains. It was not until I finished eating the "eggs" that Mom revealed I had just eaten some hog brains.

I remember the unconditional love and support Mom gave to each member of her family. She was the glue that kept our family together. I have never known a more unselfish, caring, and loving person. Her kindness and giving ways made her extra special. The whole neighborhood knew where to go if they needed something. Whether it was money, a babysitter, a cup of sugar, flour, etc., they knew whom to turn to: my mom.

I thank God for allowing her to be home for her three children and not having to work. I think if we had more of this today, we would lose less of our black children to jails and drugs. With my mom's spiritual guidance and love, we did not fall victim to the drugs and crime that surrounded us in those Southeast, Washington, D.C. neighborhoods.

— John Derwin Jackson

The memories I have of my mother are many. Of course, I am her oldest child and experienced a lot of good times with her. She was a very loving and caring wife, mother, grandmother, sister, and aunt. I remember how my mother was very giving of herself and would do anything to help someone. Her smile was warm and friendly, and of course, I see it every day when I smile at myself in the mirror. She was a very devoted church member and always made us go to church when we didn't want to. But I thank God that she did! Attending church as a child, you don't really understand some things, and most of the time you're not really paying attention. But unknowingly to you and for some reason, when you get older you find that those things taught to you in church have taken root and have stayed with you for life. They say that if you raise a child up in the way that they should go, they won't fall far from it. My mother knew this through her faith in God. I remember when I was about thirteen or fourteen, I was having a lot of nightmares about Satan. I had a dream that Satan was trying to take my soul and destroy me. I believed that I had seen him sitting next to my bed smiling at me as if to say, "You are going to be mine." I got up and quickly ran into my mother and father's bedroom and told my mother what happened to me. She told me to come into her bed, and she quickly grabbed her Bible and started reading. After she read several Scriptures to me, I felt a lot better. She then sent me to my room with a Bible and told me to pray. I can say that since that night I have not seen or heard from Satan! I'm so glad my momma prayed for me.

When my mother passed, a lot of my co-workers and supervisors said to me, "I didn't know your mother, but I know she was a wonderful and beautiful woman because of the person you are." That gave me comfort because it was at that time I began to realize that her job was well done. I also realized that we all would be OK because she left us with so many values to help get us through life. Her legacy will live on.

— *Thomas Pernell Jackson*

Chapter 41 – Alzheimer's Disease:
An Unexpected Visitor

In July 2002, we gathered at Mama's home to celebrate her eighty-fifth birthday and MacArthur's sixtieth birthday. Family members traveled from Rhode Island, Connecticut, Virginia, and Maryland. Everyone was joyful. There was singing, readings, and lots of hugs and laughter. Mama was busy strutting here and there. She was the queen not only for the day, but whenever she gathered with family.

MacArthur had recently been diagnosed with Alzheimer's disease. We were stunned. MacArthur was too young to have a memory problem, we said. Then somebody let the "cat out of the bag" as Mama likes to say whenever family secrets escape from their hiding places. We heard that the disease ran in the family on Mama's side. No details. No discussion. There were whispers that barely could be heard, and the listener was unable to make out what was being said.

Everyone was troubled over MacArthur having Alzheimer's disease. No one had recognized any signs of the disease. It seemed to have just shown up without a hint.

A few years later, we became undone upon learning that Alzheimer's disease had entered the life of Saul. Joyce, Saul, Clifford, and I had spent two weeks together. Nothing seemed out of place. Just prior to leaving for T. F. Green Airport for the return trip back to Connecticut, Saul began to ask me every few minutes what time our flight was. I would give him the information each time but suddenly said, "I have told you the time. Why you keep asking me?" Upon arrival at the airport, Saul said he was not feeling well. We thought he had come down with the flu. After a two-hour flight, he needed assistance, as he was barely able to walk. He entered W. W. Backus Hospital and remained in the critical care unit for two weeks. Saul recovered but was never the same.

Looking back, we can see little things that should have been clues that the disease had entered the life of another loved one. For example, Saul began to lose his ability to fix things he previously could fix easily. He went to the mall in search of me instead of going to my house after being notified by the security company that the alarm system had gone off.

Upon hearing of Saul's diagnosis, our family was heartbroken. However, Saul continued to travel with family members to Hawaii, Florida, the Berkshires, New Hampshire, and Newport, Rhode Island. His condition worsened. Saul passed on October 28, 2007, and it was tough on everyone. He was known for his physical and spiritual strength. He and Joyce were generous, kind, and supportive of family members. He is fondly remembered as "King Solomon" and full of wisdom, as was his grandfather Solomon Stone.

I gave the following eulogy at Saul's funeral:

"Solomon Wesley Bell was born of ordinary means but became an extraordinary person. He was proud of his namesake, Solomon Stone, his grandfather—who was a wise man, a person who respected himself and others, and demanded no less from them. These traits and others became a part of Saul's persona. When he strolled, he walked tall and erect, exuding confidence. He did not take stuff from anyone. If you start it, be sure you can outrun his left hand.

"Saul said it pays to always respect old people. He is held in high esteem by many elderly people because he never forgets to visit them, bring produce from his garden, share the results of his fishing trips, or just sit and talk with them through good or bad times. His relationships were special and enduring.

"Saul understood the importance of economics. He refused to be weighed down by credit cards, which he likened to the chains of slavery. He used credit cards, but never paid a late charge and never had a balance more than thirty days old. He enjoyed my bringing him coffee and a pastry every morning. Each morning, Saul thanked me while eating, and laughing that he would not pay Starbuck prices when he could get McDonald's for much less.

"Saul had a deep love for family and friends. He was always there in time of need or celebrations. He and Joyce could be counted upon to attend celebrations, send gifts to graduates and newlyweds. He was proud of the many accomplishments of family members. Saul loved to watch the children swim in hotel pools. 'I bet you the hotel has never had that many black people in its pool at one time,' he would chuckle. He would recall the days as youngsters when we had only the creek for swimming, which was filled with snakes and other critters. Oh, he was a proud man—like his Grandpa Saul.

"Saul was not a follower. So, when family members assumed that he wanted a dinner for his sixtieth birthday like Lottie Mae and Freddie, he replied, 'No, I want to go on a cruise. What!!! People can't afford a cruise. They don't have to go. Just send me.' In March of 1999, for his sixtieth birthday, he sailed on Royal Caribbean Majesty of the Seas. It was indeed appropriate for 'King Solomon,' whom we found strolling on the deck smiling, saying, 'This is sooo beautiful.' Gifts showed up every night on his bed. On his birthday, a beautiful medallion appeared, and it was the talk of the dining room. Who are you and how do you rate this? 'My name is Solomon Bell, and my grandfather is Solomon Stone.' He received royal treatment. And things were never the same.

"Along came Jermaine, about six months old, Joyce and Saul's first great-grandchild, to live with them while his mother Tina went to Iraq and it was perfect timing for Saul. He gave Jermaine his undivided attention, Granddaddy's little buddy. It was heartwarming to watch Saul changing Jermaine's diapers and feeding him. According to his granddaddy Saul, Jermaine was the smartest baby in the world. Just give him a toy, and he would figure out how it works. Saul showed this baby how to build muscles and be strong. One day, Jermaine picked up a weight and strolled across the floor with the ease of carrying a banana. Joyce and I screamed while Saul roared with laughter. On another occasion, Jermaine decided to throw a punch like Granddaddy taught him. This time Saul's nose was his target. Jermaine coming into Saul's life brought joy to Saul that we all shared.

"The times we share with Solomon will never be forgotten. He was born of ordinary means, but he lived an extraordinary life. We are going to miss him—the laughter, the teasing, the challenging arm wrestling, and growing a better garden. Today our hearts are sad, as he is no longer physically with us. I am reminded of Grandpa Solomon Stone's words when I was experiencing sadness as a young girl. He would say, "Granddaughter, you are going to cross the River Jordan." It was years before I understood that he was saying everything was going to be all right. Saul has crossed the River Jordan, and everything is all right. He did not cross alone. He carried us in his heart. Everything is all right. Saul is still with us in our hearts as we stand on the shore of life. Everything will be all right. We, too, will cross the River Jordan. Everything will be all right."

After Saul's death, David announced that he was having memory problems, but he was not claiming Alzheimer's disease. David had a brilliant mind and a good memory. He worked in inventory, and many people were amazed at his ability to retrieve information. David was proud, also. Then one day, his ability to remember began to slip away. Eventually, he entered a care facility, where he remained until his death on November 25, 2017.

In the spring of 2009, Freddie went to visit Mama. It was a joyful trip, as he got a chance to spend time with Mama, Aunt Geneva, Cousin Norvice, and other family members. It took a lot of planning for Freddie to make the trip, and a caretaker had to accompany him. He returned to Rhode Island filled with joy, and hope that he would be able to repeat the journey, but his health declined, and he was unable to return to South Carolina to visit Mama. Freddie died in the early spring of 2011. Freddie was never diagnosed with Alzheimer's disease. No one dared hint of his being affected by Alzheimer's disease. However, I believe that Freddie's behavior at times suggested that his brain was being attacked. He did not attend Saul's memorial service in Connecticut. This was unusual behavior for Freddie, considering he and Saul were so close.

MacArthur remained at home for fifteen years during his journey with Alzheimer's disease. His wife Jessie and their four children, Reecy, Dwayne, Wade, and Darryl, helped with his care. As the grandchildren got older, they joined in to help. MacArthur had influenced their career decisions. Granddaughter Alecia is on track to becoming a nurse; she was about age five when she began to feed him dinner. Jessie says that without the help of the children, MacArthur would not have been able to live at home. It took a lot of work, commitment, and professional services. MacArthur died in the winter of 2014.

Mama was nearing ninety when memory loss came into her life. We attributed it to normal aging. During her journey with Alzheimer's disease and dementia, she was lovingly cared for by Josephine, who became Mama's primary caretaker. Mama passed on December 6, 2011, at age ninety-four.

After settling Mama's estate, Josephine announced that she too had memory issues. She is being cared for at a residential facility. She gave up a promising career to care for Mama and says she has no regrets.

Alberta cared for her husband Grant, a brilliant man who served his country. He and Alberta established a ministry to help others at home and abroad. They traveled to Africa and other places to lend their support. Again, Alzheimer's disease arrived with barely a notice, yet it has drastically changed his life and the lives of loved ones. He died on April 7, 2018.

Our awareness of this disease has become front and center in our lives. Our children, grandchildren, and great-grandchildren know that it devastates lives. The younger generation has begun to seek information about it and wonder aloud how it can be stopped.

The threat of Alzheimer's disease hangs over our heads like a dark threatening cloud with thunder and lightning. Why has this disease not entered the lives of Mama's and Daddy's siblings and their children, to the best of our knowledge? On the other hand, there could be many a "cat in the bag" out there.

Mama taught us to always take our troubles to the Lord. We pray that this enemy of the mind will be stopped in its tracks and not visit our family again. I believe Alzheimer's disease is just lurking around my door and taking its time to spring upon me. As I celebrate my eighty-first birthday, I am very mindful of the disease. Family and friends are forever telling me they are waiting for me to complete this book. Alzheimer's disease can leap upon its victim seemingly with only a moment's notice. When I look at a familiar face, and cannot call the person by the name I have been calling for years, I think to myself, "It is just a matter of time before Alzheimer's disease comes for me." I pray the encounter will be brief.

Epilogue

I was born a girl child. Like my mother, I had dreams beyond the circumstances of my birth. My Lord! My Lord! What a journey it was to pursue my dreams while tasting the bitter weeds along the way. My parents began their life together having only their love and a determination to provide for their children.

At an early age, I encountered racism, sexism, and poverty. I even began to question religion as it was being taught. I questioned how some people had and others did not, but all had the same God, how year after year, Santa Claus left very little in our stockings, but left our neighbors' children many toys and goodies. As a young person, I learned "you do not question God's work."

Before the age of twelve, I witnessed an adult cousin being beaten by two white policemen in Ridgeway, South Carolina. I told Mama that my cousin was not doing anything; he was just talking to me. Her reply stills rings in my head: "They got the power."

When the U.S. Supreme Court desegregated the schools, I watched how quickly new schools were built. Suddenly black children were being transported to the new schools on buses that picked them up early in the morning. The young children were dropped off at the school, but they were not allowed to enter because it was before regular school hours. The bus would go and get another load of children while the children shivered in the cold outside and cried.

I asked the high school boys to build a human pyramid, open the window, and unlock the doors to let the little children in the school. It was not long before the authorities showed up and threatened to arrest the boys should they enter the school again. I was home sick the day that happened, which I believe saved my life. Some students were glad I was not present, and others said, "If you were here, we would have stoned the police." It was then I learned I had a voice people would listen to. I also recalled Mama's warning: "They got the power." Throwing rocks was not the answer. Years later, I chose to join the NAACP to work for change.

I moved from South Carolina to Norwich, Connecticut, in the spring of 1957 with the belief that there was an opportunity for jobs and that there was no racism. I believed that people were free to eat and work where they chose, and I was ready to enjoy the freedoms and equality of living in the North.

It was not long before I discovered I had not arrived at the Promised Land. Norwich was not a place free of prejudice and discrimination. The Westside was where newly arrived blacks lived. It was hard for blacks to find housing outside of the Westside. Attempts to move to other areas were met with resistance. When you showed up to see an apartment, you were told it was taken, while whites who came later were told it was still available.

As a single mother and head of household, I was asked for my state welfare identification when I took my son to the William W. Backus Hospital, and I objected to the assumption that I was on welfare. When I complained to the president of the hospital, he stated he would not change this practice to ask first for an insurance card. At the time, I lived in Oakwood Knoll, a low-income public housing project. The majority of the units were female head of household. I filed a complaint with the Connecticut Commission on Human Rights and Opportunities because I thought the practice was discriminatory

Looking back, I have been an activist in civil rights, the arts, and community work, and continue to champion the cause of equality and equity. Two years after my arrival in Norwich, Ellis Walter Ruley, an artist and black resident, was found dead under mysterious circumstances. A book about his life and work, *Discovering Ellis Ruley*, by Glenn Smith, was published in 1995, and Ellis Walter Ruley became nationally known. He was a self-taught artist. He painted with common house paint and sold his paintings to provide for his family. In 2015, the City of Norwich created the Ellis Walter Ruley Committee, of which I am proud to be member. The mission is to create a park and sanctuary on the homestead property and an annual festival to commemorate his life.

At age eighty-one, I look back not in anger but in gratitude. My experience helped shaped who I am today. It helped me survive and teach others how to overcome challenging circumstances. Today, our children, and their children, are achieving in ways that once were thought impossible. Our mother was always inspiring us to work for what we want and not depend upon other people. "When you do a job, do it right," she urged. Mama learned from her daddy that you held your head high and you did the best job possible you could, even if it was carrying a slop jar. There was no shame in doing a good job. It was a matter of pride in your work and pride in self. Your quality of work represented you.

Mama said to always put God in front of you and the Devil behind you, and you will triumph over evil. Mama never strayed from her faith in God. She never shouted in church or got down on her knees to pray. Mama said she did not have to, because "God knows my heart." She loved going to church and equally loved going to the juke joints. She took us with her. Mama loved to dance, and drink a little spirit, but always kept a level head. We sat at a table and watched her dance. All the while, Mama kept her eyes on us. Should friend or foe walk up to our table for a conversation, Mama was on them as quickly as a chicken hawk when a hen leaves their little ones alone for a second. No one dared to engage in a conversation with Mama's children without her permission.

Mama told me she was inspired by her grandfather George Washington Goins. He was a fun-loving man. According to Mama, he told her he was going to serve the Lord and the Devil too because he did not know where he may land. Wherever he landed, he would be greeted with "You've been a good and faithful servant."

Mama has been an inspiration and anchor that has kept our family on a steady course. She held the young lovingly and praised them generously. She spoke to them sweetly. She also never spared the rod if necessary.

Like my mother, I had dreams of fairness and justice for all regardless of race, sex, age, or religion. It has been my life journey toward that goal. Today, our family embraces each other lovingly. We have blended across the spectrum, yet we are one in spirit. We are family. Today, we have attorneys, college graduates, law enforcement officers, health care workers, and others in a variety of work. Our next generations will touch the sky and contribute to humankind worldwide. Our young family members are seeking positions that once seemed like a dream. Mama inspired generations with her love and wisdom. The path was not easy, but the results speak volumes about her impact. A mother's love continues to inspire generations.

In Loving Memory of Estelle Stone Bell.

END.

Great Grandmother
Charity Kirkland Goins

Great Grandfather George Goins

Grandma Ella Goins Stone

Grandpa Solomon Stone

Great Grandfather
George Belton

Great Grandparents War-
ren and Nora Roach Bell

Uncle Albert Bell

Grandpa Joe Bell, Sr. and
Grandson Joe Belton

Uncle George Bell

Estelle Stone Bell

Joe Bell, Jr.

Clyburn Scott Jr.

Lottie Mae Bell Scott

Rock Hill Baptist Church in Longtown, SC

Former Mount Olive Baptist Church in Longtown, SC

Mount Joshua Church in Longtown, SC

Martha Bell's Wedding in Washington, DC in 1958

Lottie Mae and Dorothy Mae at Graduation from Fairfield High School in 1956

Brother Solomon with Lottie Mae at Graduation from the University of Connecticut in 1984

Cynthia and Monel Ruiz Wedding in 2012 "Jimping the Broom"

Ayja'leigha Dortch with her Aunt Angela at High School Graduation in 2014

Family Social at the Home of Alberta and Charles Dortch

Estelle Stone Bell with her eight children

Freddie Bell with grandson "A Fishing Tradition"

Lottie Mae and Uncle Prince

Visiting with Cousins in Washington, DC in 2015

Solomon Stone's 101st Birthday Celebration with daughters and granddaughter Josephine

Norvice, Aunt Geneva and Lottie Mae

Vernell Stone "Aunt Baby Ruth"

Alice White, Local Historian

Cousins Alberta, Nell, Lottie Mae and Bea

Nancy Belton Ross Jackson, Cousin

Margaret Kirkland Murphy, Cousin

Clyburn III, Lottie Mae, Clyburn Jr., and
Estelle Bell at 1997 Bell Family reunion

Lillian Blondell and Family

Clifford Carter Jr., and Lottie Mae in 2016

Bell Family Reunion

Lottie Mae with three generations at
her 75th birthday celebration

Lottie Mae and Son Clyburn Jr.
staying connected with the earth

Jean, Lottie Mae, Willie O. and Georgy   Joe Louis Griffin and Ben Bush

Miss Maggie Derry, Teacher at Mount Olive School
and Antioch Baptist Church Sunday School and students

Cousin Lottie Mae   Cousin Luvenia

Deacons Moses and Dwayne Bell at
Mount Olive Baptist Church following
in the footsteps of their ancestors

James Bell, Esq., son of Attorney
Josephine Bell Patton

Lottie Mae and Niece "Reecy"
Thompson "An Emerging Matriarch"

Terri's Family host
Christmas Party in Hawaii

Lottie Mae with Nieces at her 80th
Birthday Celebration

Lottie Mae with Nephews at her 80th
Birthday Celebration

FAMILY ANCESTRY OF ESTELLE STONE BELL AND JOE BELL, JR.

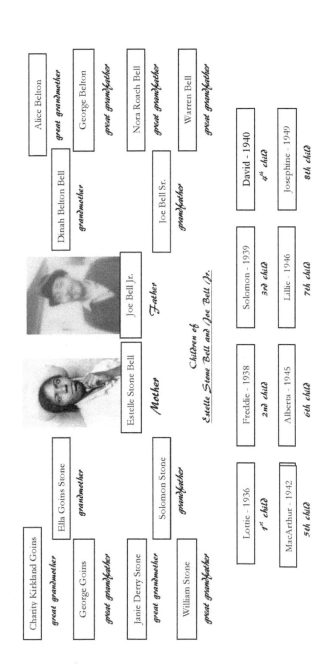

Charity Kirkland Goins
great grandmother

Ella Goins Stone
grandmother

George Goins
great grandfather

Janie Derry Stone
great grandmother

Solomon Stone
grandfather

William Stone
great grandfather

Estelle Stone Bell
Mother

Joe Bell Jr.
Father

Alice Belton
great grandmother

George Belton
great grandfather

Dinah Belton Bell
grandmother

Nora Roach Bell
great grandmother

Joe Bell Sr.
grandfather

Warren Bell
great grandfather

Children of Estelle Stone Bell and Joe Bell Jr.

Lottie - 1936
1st child

Freddie - 1938
2nd child

Solomon - 1939
3rd child

David - 1940
4th child

MacArthur - 1942
5th child

Alberta - 1945
6th child

Lillie - 1946
7th child

Josephine - 1949
8th child

CPSIA information can be obtained
at www.ICGtesting.com
Printed in the USA
BVHW04s1551220818
525176BV00032B/242/P